DE

& CORN

WALL

Travel with Marco Polo Insider Tips

INSIDER TIP
Your shortcut
to a great
experience

MARCO POLO
TOP HIGHLIGHTS

EDEN PROJECT ⭐1
Different climates from around the world are recreated inside huge "biomes" at this eco-park.
📷 *Tip: Photograph the domes from above when the sun is shining.*

➤ p. 42, West Cornwall

ST MICHAEL'S MOUNT ⭐2
Just like the one in Normandy: this monastery off the coast of Cornwall is the Mont-Saint-Michel's smaller sibling.
📷 *Tip: Take a shot in the early morning or at sunset when the light is at its most magical – even better with a boat in the foreground.*

➤ p. 50, West Cornwall

ISLES OF SCILLY ⭐3
Caribbean vibes off the coast of England: these remote islands are a holiday paradise.

➤ p. 53, West Cornwall

TATE ST IVES ⭐4
This branch of the famous Tate Gallery displays amazing art right by the beach.
📷 *Tip: Head to the café terrace and point your camera to the northeast over the beach, with a few house roofs in frame.*

➤ p. 56, West Cornwall

NEWQUAY'S BEACHES ⭐5
The beaches along the coast at Newquay stretch for almost 10km (photo) – perfect for surfers and non-surfers alike.

➤ p. 58, West Cornwall

TINTAGEL CASTLE ⭐6
These castle ruins on the coast are a sight to behold – even if you don't believe in the legend of King Arthur …

➤ p. 74, East Cornwall

DARTMOUTH STEAM RAILWAY ⭐ 7

Travel like Miss Marple: take a steam train through the beautiful landscape between Paignton and Kingswear.

📷 *Tip: On bends, you can get a great photo with both the train and the scenery in shot – but watch out for tree branches!*

➤ p. 88, South Devon

BARBICAN ⭐ 9

You expect to see pirates waiting round every corner – Plymouth's old port harks back to times gone by.

➤ p. 91, South Devon

GREENWAY ⭐ 8

This romantic house, complete with boathouse and riverside views, and surrounded by magnificent gardens, was the summer residence of famous crime writer Agatha Christie.

📷 *Tip: From parts of the circular path, you can get a great shot of the River Dart.*

➤ p. 89, South Devon

DARTMOOR ⭐ 10

This mystical moorland is one of England's most beautiful national parks.

📷 *Tip: Sit on one of the stones at Hound Tor and have your picture taken from a distance, preferably with a cloudy sky in the background.*

➤ p. 94, South Devon

CONTENTS

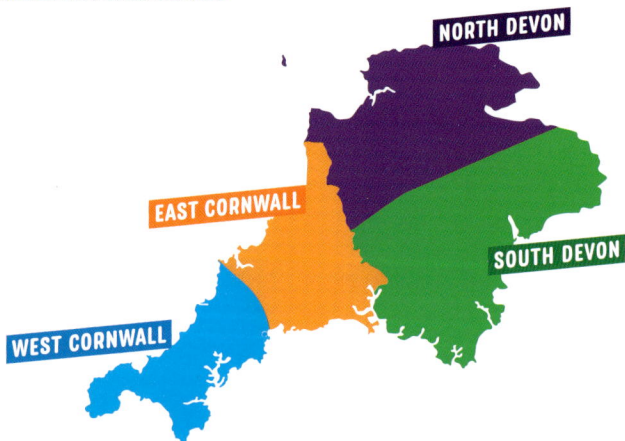

NORTH DEVON
EAST CORNWALL
SOUTH DEVON
WEST CORNWALL

36 REGIONAL OVERVIEW

38 WEST CORNWALL
42 St Austell & around
43 Truro & around   45 Falmouth &
around   47 Lizard & around
49 Penzance & around   53 Isles of
Scilly   55 St Ives   57 Newquay &
around

60 EAST CORNWALL
64 Launceston & around
65 Liskeard & around
67 Bodmin & around   69 Fowey &
around   71 Padstow & around
74 Tintagel & around

76 SOUTH DEVON
80 Exeter & around
82 Exmouth & around   85 Torquay
& around   88 Dartmouth & around
91 Plymouth & around
94 Dartmoor & around

98 NORTH DEVON
102 Exmoor & around
104 Ilfracombe & around
107 Barnstaple & around
109 Great Torrington & around

CONTENTS

MARCO POLO TOP HIGHLIGHTS

2   Top 10 highlights

BEST OF DEVON & CORNWALL

8   ... when it rains
9   ... on a budget
10   ... with children
11   ... classic experiences

GET TO KNOW DEVON & CORNWALL

14   Discover Devon & Cornwall
17   At a glance
18   Understand Devon & Cornwall
21   True or false?

EATING, SHOPPING, SPORT

26   Eating & drinking
30   Shopping
32   Sport & activities

MARCO POLO REGIONS

36   Regional overview

DISCOVERY TOURS

112 On the trail of Agatha Christie
115 Hiking on the South West Coast Path
117 Castles & gardens

GOOD TO KNOW

120 **HOLIDAY BASICS**
Arrival, Getting around, Festivals & events, Emergencies, Essentials, Weather

130 **HOLIDAY VIBES**
Books, films, music & blogs

132 **TRAVEL PURSUIT**
The Marco Polo holiday quiz

134 **INDEX & CREDITS**

136 **DOS AND DON'TS**
How to avoid slip-ups & blunders

(⊙) Plan your visit

£–£££ Price categories

(*) Premium rate phone number

🍴 Eating/drinking

🛍 Shopping

🍸 Going out

🏖 Top beaches

🌂 Rainy day activities

🐷 Budget activities

👪 Family activities

🚩 Classic experiences

(📖 A2) Refers to the removable pull-out map
(📖 a2) Refers to the inset map on the pull-out map
(📖 0) Location is not on the pull-out map

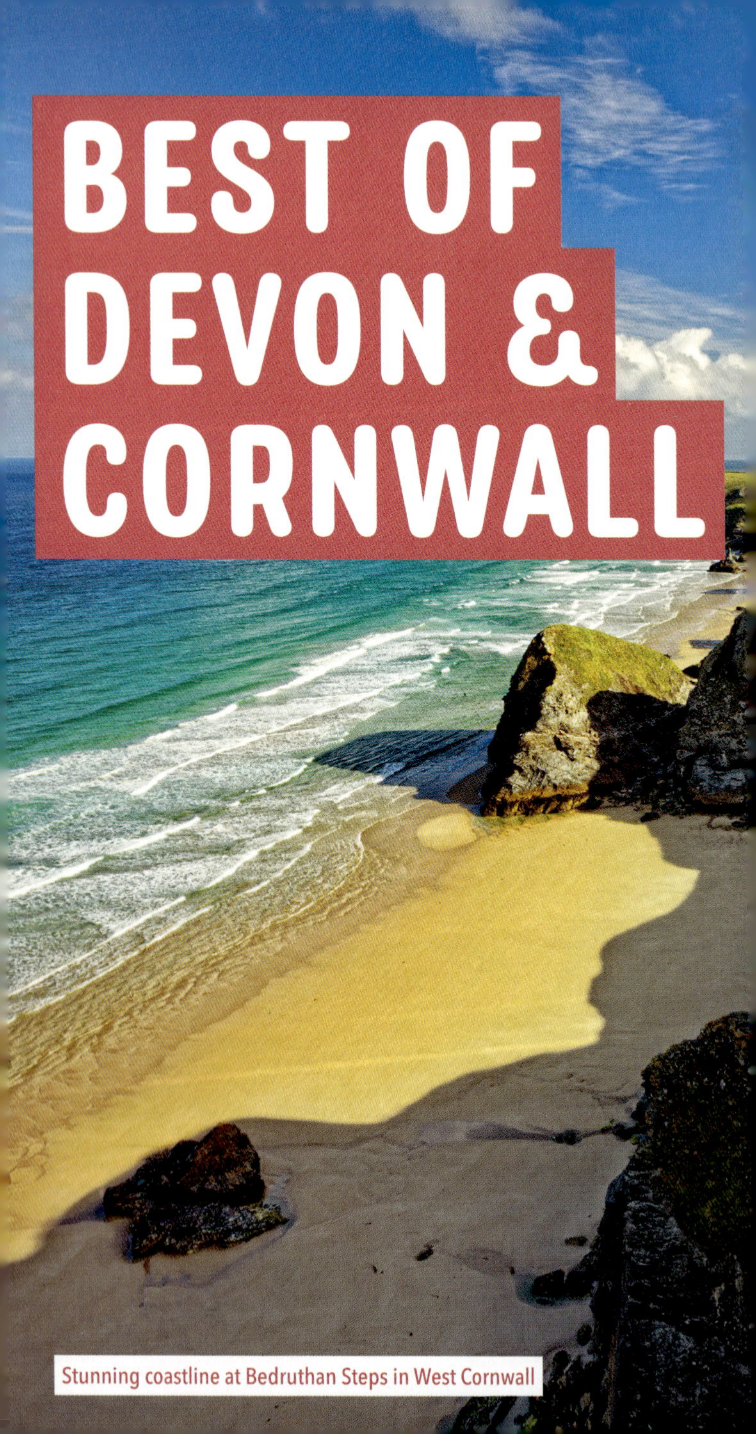

Stunning coastline at Bedruthan Steps in West Cornwall

BEST WHEN IT RAINS

ACTIVITIES TO BRIGHTEN YOUR DAY

THE EARTH'S CLIMATIC ZONES

The *Eden Project* (photo) recreates the earth's climate zones under huge covered biomes – but without the rain, though some do have high humidity. Where else in England can you experience temperatures of 30°C in winter?

➤ p. 42, West Cornwall

ART FROM LONDON

Who says you have to travel to London to see wonderful art? The Tate, one of the country's top collections, displays masterpieces at stunning *Tate St Ives* – indoors and dry!

➤ p. 56, West Cornwall

JUMP INTO WARM WATER

You can forget about the rain and spend the entire day at *Leisure World* in Newquay. It's also fabulous for children!

➤ p. 58, West Cornwall

VISIT THE CAVES

Near Torquay, in *Kents Cavern*, nobody worries about the weather – the temperatures are constant here. This is the oldest cave system in Britain, inhabited by humans many thousands of years ago.

➤ p. 85, South Devon

STARE THE FISH IN THE EYE

The *National Marine Aquarium* in Plymouth not only displays fish from all over the world, but also has the deepest tank in the country.

➤ p. 92, South Devon

SHOP FOR A BARGAIN

Why not grab yourself a bargain? *Affinity Devon* outlet mall in Bideford offers big-name brands at cut prices. You'll forget about the bad weather in no time!

➤ p. 110, North Devon

BEST 🐷 ON A BUDGET

FOR SMALLER WALLETS

BEHIND THE SCENES AT A DAIRY FARM

Jersey cows produce particularly creamy milk, perfect for making ice cream. On *Roskilly's* farm near St Keverne, you can have a look behind the scenes – free of charge.

➤ p. 48, West Cornwall

MUSEUMS FOR FREE

Many museums charge hefty admission fees, particularly for specially curated exhibitions. At *Lawrence House* in Launceston you can learn all about Cornwall's history, and it won't cost you a penny. Donations welcome.

➤ p. 64, East Cornwall

CITY WALKS

Exeter's *Red Coat Guided Tours* run city walks that everybody can join for free. There are at least two walks daily, starting from the cathedral.

➤ p. 80, South Devon

PUB SPECIALS

Dining out can get pricey, but many pubs have special offers, either on specific days or all the time – you can often get a free drink with your meal or two dishes for the price of one. One such pub is *The Imperial* in Exeter.

➤ p. 81, South Devon

HISTORY ON THE HOUSE

Devon and Cornwall are strewn with centuries-old buildings, and *Lydford Castle* is one of the few medieval ruins that you can visit for free.

➤ p. 97, South Devon

BEST
WITH CHILDREN

FUN FOR YOUNG & OLD

RARE ANIMALS
Newquay Zoo is primarily focused on breeding rare animals. Over 130 species are found here, including lions and monkeys, and there is a special play area for children.

➤ p. 57, West Cornwall

FULL STEAM AHEAD
There's fun to be had at *Lappa Valley Steam Railway*: ride a steam train around this former mine or play on a wooden toy version and pretend to be the train driver. Children will have a great time here – and you can even go canoeing.

➤ p. 59, West Cornwall

MINI FISHING VILLAGE
The little fishing village of Polperro is so lovely that its residents have built it again in miniature. At *Polperro Model Village* you can get a unique view of the place.

➤ p. 67, East Cornwall

ADRENALIN KICK
Hang out like a monkey: at *Go Ape*, near Exeter, you can swing from tree to tree, zoom through the air on a zip-wire or simply walk across the rope bridge – all safely harnessed in.

➤ p. 82, South Devon

WATER PARK WITH A SEA VIEW
Splashdown Quaywest, south of Torquay, is Britain's biggest outdoor waterpark. Splash into the water from its eight slides with views over Torbay!

➤ p. 87, South Devon

DINOSAURS IN DEVON
Fancy seeing some prehistoric creatures? At *Woodlands* theme park, you can follow dinosaur tracks, soar through the air on a giant swing and zoom down slides.

➤ p. 89, South Devon

CLASSIC EXPERIENCES

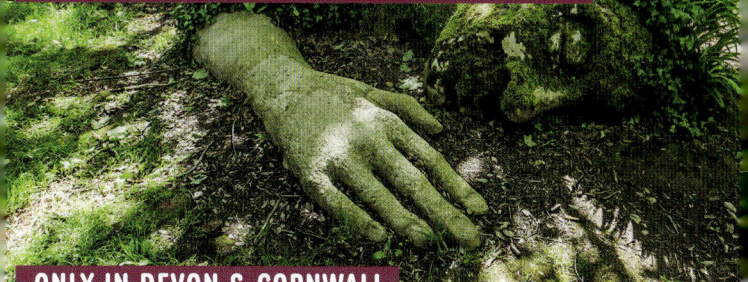

ONLY IN DEVON & CORNWALL

GARDENS GALORE

Landscaped gardens are almost compulsory for any large country estate in Devon and Cornwall – after all, plenty of plants grow here that don't flourish elsewhere in the UK. The *Lost Gardens of Heligan* (photo) are a particularly wonderful example.

➤ p. 43, West Cornwall

BEACHES AND WATER SPORTS

Water sports are a way of life in Devon and Cornwall. The coastline offers numerous beaches for bathing, surfing and diving – particularly popular spots are *the beaches of Newquay* in Cornwall and *Exmouth Beach* in Devon.

➤ p. 58, West Cornwall, p. 84, South Devon

AN AUTHENTIC CREAM TEA

No trip to Devon or Cornwall is complete without a genuine cream tea. But what goes on the scone first, the clotted cream or the strawberry jam? Start your research at the *Chapel Café* in Port Isaac, near Padstow.

➤ p. 73, East Cornwall

A PINT IN THE PUB

What would Britain be without pubs? A lot less friendly, that's for sure. Meet for a pint in the local pub and take the opportunity to chat with the locals. For example, at *The Castle* in Porlock, a little village to the north of Exmoor.

➤ p. 103, North Devon

HIKING ALONG THE COAST

The *South West Coast Path* circles the whole of the Devon and Cornwall coast. It's a great opportunity to don your hiking boots and explore the coast. You don't need to complete the entire route – why not pick a short section to walk along?

➤ p. 111, North Devon

GET TO KNOW DEVON & CORNWALL

East Devon with a sea view: deck chairs on Beer Beach

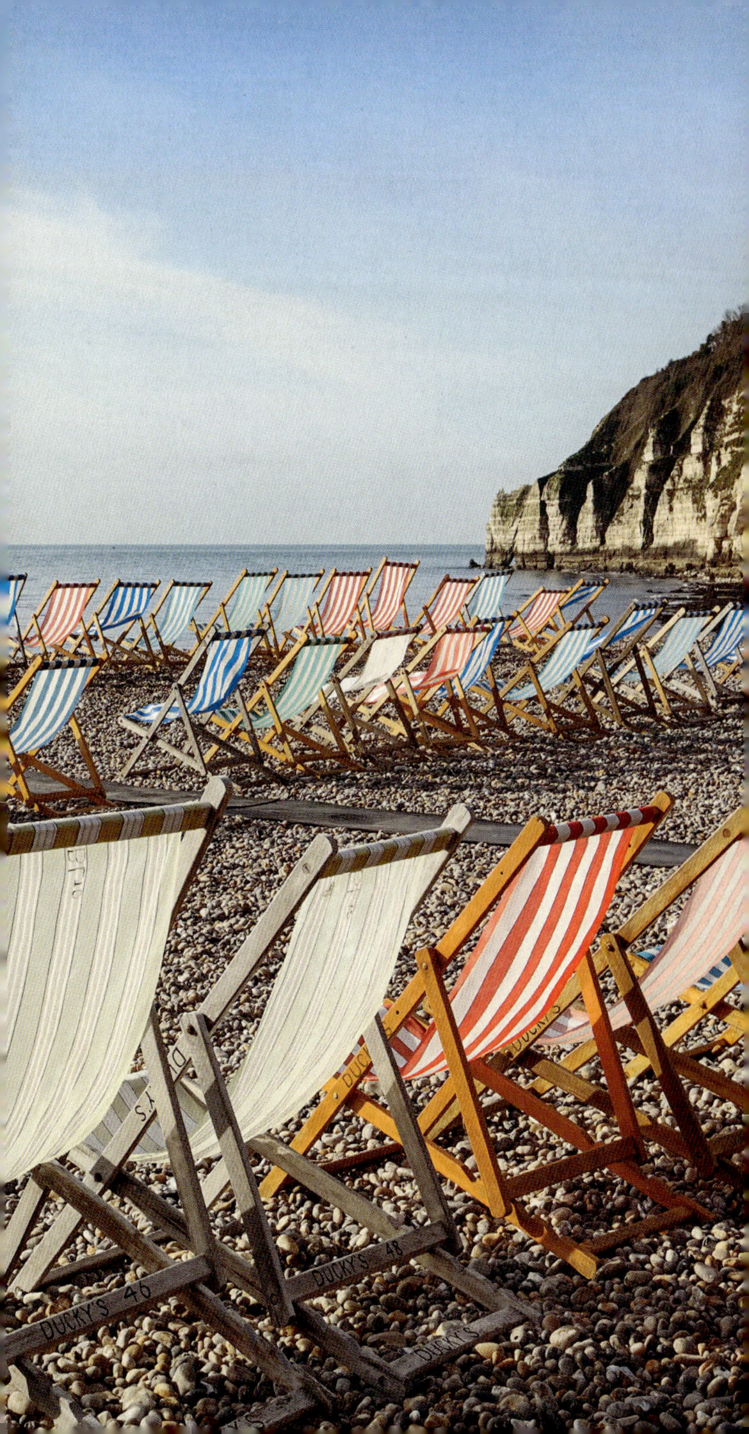
DUCKY'S 46
DUCKY'S 48

DISCOVER DEVON & CORNWALL

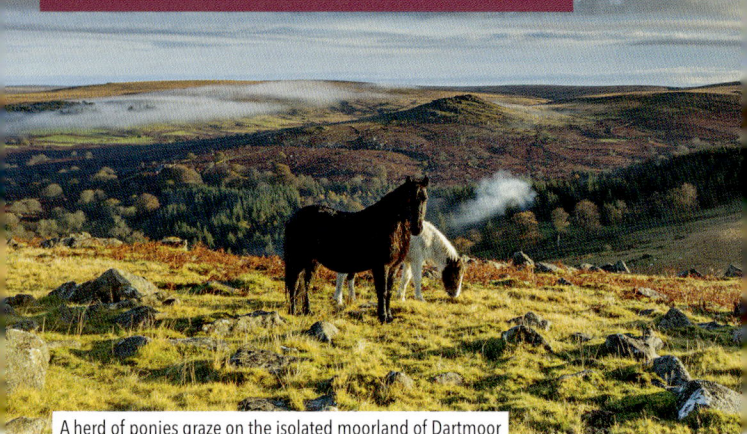

A herd of ponies graze on the isolated moorland of Dartmoor

Are you in the mood for beaches and surfing? Or would you prefer history and nature? Do you like trendy bars or rustic pubs? Modern hotels with infinity pools or stately houses with landscaped gardens and afternoon tea? Either way, welcome to Devon and Cornwall – a corner of the British Isles where everyone can find a holiday to suit their taste.

PALM TREES IN THE GARDEN

Both these southwestern counties perfectly reflect the natural beauty of the British countryside, offering abundant architectural treasures and a people who are unique to this part of the island. And if that weren't enough, despite rumours to the contrary, the weather is often pleasant. Thanks to the effect of the Gulf Stream, the temperatures rarely fall below zero – even palm trees grow in the

6000 BCE
Early human settlements are established on Dartmoor (long before that, Neanderthals lived in Kents Cavern, near Torquay)

CE 43
The Romans occupy Britain. They remain until 440 AD

400
The name "Kernow" (Cornwall) is first recorded

500
Tthe Romano-Celtic populace battle with the Angles and Saxons, forming the basis of the legends of King Arthur

1620
The *Mayflower* sets out from Plymouth with the first English settlers departing for America

front gardens. Summers are warm, but not too hot. That's why Devon and Cornwall count among the most popular holiday regions in the United Kingdom.

DREAMING, SURFING, PARTYING

Devon and Cornwall's rich literary history has lured many travellers here. You can discover picture-postcard scenery around almost every corner. But this is just a tiny part of what life is like here.

Newquay in southwest Cornwall has long since emerged as one of Europe's top surfing spots. During the summer, surfers from all over the world are enticed here to conquer the waves.

Many areas of Devon and Cornwall have more young people than you might think. Devon's county town of Exeter is a university city with an excellent reputation for research. International scholars are attracted here from many different countries. While the idyllic old town around the majestic cathedral is regarded as one of England's top attractions, a lively student scene has also developed with, of course, a suitably buzzing nightlife – there are plenty of cool pubs between the station and the town centre.

Life in the countryside is much quieter. In central Devon, on Exmoor, Dartmoor and along the Cornish coast, time has apparently stood still. Local retailers have held their ground particularly well here. There are numerous small shops offering all kinds of trinkets along with fishing rods or a pint of milk. The locals call these shops quirky, and most visitors are attracted here precisely because things *are* quirky.

1833 The building of the Great Western Railway brings tourists to Devon and Cornwall in greater numbers

1998 South Crofty mine closes, ending 4,000 years of mining in Cornwall

2016 Britons vote by a narrow majority to leave the EU, with Devon and Cornwall largely supportive of Brexit

2023 Cornwall Airport in Newquay becomes the UK's first space airport. However, the inaugural launch in January fails

REVIVING THE CORNISH LANGUAGE

The people in the southwest are generally welcoming to visitors. At the same time, there is a strong regional pride, and in Cornwall you will often see a black flag with a white cross – the Cornish flag – flying from houses or stuck to car windows. Cornish, a Celtic language that had all but died out, is now enjoying a revival.

COMFORTABLE LUXURY IN BOUTIQUE HOTELS

Devon and Cornwall became popular tourist destinations in the 19th century. Those who live in the southwest have long taken pride in the fact that visitors love to travel here. This might explain the attitude of some hotel and restaurant owners, who rest on their laurels and believe that modernisation is unnecessary. Even today, the wind still whistles through the single-glazed windows in some places and, in the (age-old) British tradition, some of the beds are made with sheets and a woollen blanket instead of a duvet. But the region has also attracted considerable investment from large hotel chains, who have set up new establishments with a different, more luxurious style.

PLENTY TO DISCOVER

Two unique landmarks are also situated in Cornwall: England's southernmost Lizard Point and the westernmost landmark at Land's End. Both lie in fabulous coastal areas, although unfortunately they are often overrun with tourists. It's best to leave the crowds behind and explore the coastal path.

There is hardly a square inch that isn't suitable for hiking here – it is well worth walking along the South West Coast Path, which extends just over 1,000km along the coastline, or exploring the rugged wilderness that is Dartmoor.

Alternatively, you can get away on a boat and enjoy one of the most beautiful island groups in Great Britain: the Isles of Scilly. The islands are situated at the westernmost point of England, about 45km off Land's End.

AT A GLANCE

1.7 MILLION
inhabitants

Northern Ireland: 1.8 million

772km
Devon & Cornwall section of the South West Coast Path

London to Edinburgh: 649km

10,270km²
Surface area

Northern Ireland: 14,139 km²

HIGH CLIFF NEAR BOSCASTLE:

223m

The highest cliff in Cornwall

WARMEST MONTH IN EXETER

AUGUST
21 °C

Temperature in St Ives in December: 10 °C

THERE ARE

300

beaches in Cornwall

ROSAMUNDE PILCHER NOVELS

Over 60 million copies sold worldwide

CRIME

Agatha Christie's novel *And Then There Were None* sold 100 million copies

CORNISH PASTY
120 million made every year

750 PUBS TO CHOOSE FROM IN DEVON

UNDERSTAND DEVON & CORNWALL

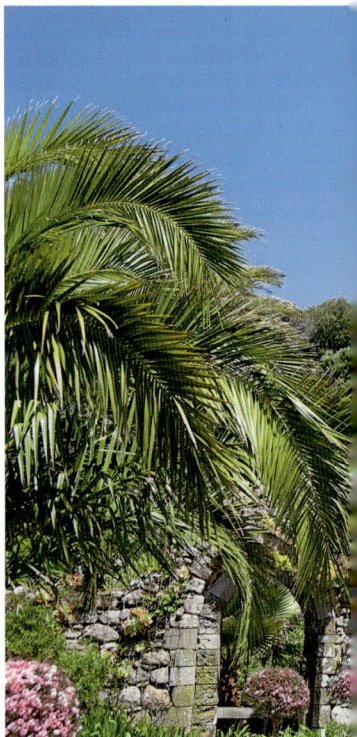

A BALMY CLIMATE

It's not all mist, rain and biting cold! Although rather unusual at these latitudes, palm trees – native to South America and the Canary Islands – seem to grow in many a front garden in Devon and Cornwall. The Gulf Stream flows past Britain's southwest coast, furnishing it with a climate that is milder than other parts of the country. It rarely snows in this region, and the temperatures in winter almost never fall below zero. Rain showers are frequent, but this is also why the grass is so green. However, constant rain is rare here, and short sharp showers are more usual. The location can also mean that, even if flooding is affecting the roads on Dartmoor, only a few miles away in Exeter the sun can be shining. You're bound to find good weather somewhere – it's just a question of tracking it down.

MAJESTIC

What must it feel like to be everywhere at once? When the British monarch goes shopping – assuming he ever does – he pays with his image, as it is featured on the coins and banknotes in the UK. When he sends a letter, he sticks himself on the envelope, because standard postage stamps feature his head. After the death of Queen Elizabeth II in 2022, it took a while for her son, King Charles III, to appear on banknotes, coins and stamps, but the substitution is now in full swing. But for all that, the monarchy doesn't play a big role in political matters. The UK maintains the tradition of a constitutional monarchy, meaning that it's the prime minister and parliament that hold the real political power.

THE LAND OF GARDENS

He is like the Shakespeare of garden and landscape design: Lancelot "Capability" Brown created the

Exotic plants at Tresco Abbey Garden

classical design for English gardens and parkland in the 18th century and is still world famous. Brown designed some 170 estates in Great Britain. No manor house or castle is complete without an artfully designed park. Several dozen designers later imitated Brown's landscaped gardens. In Devon and Cornwall there are numerous beautiful parks and gardens, such as those of Tresco Abbey or Lanhydrock. In the southwest, traditions are especially appreciated and carefully cultivated – and that includes gardens.

CHEERS!

In Devon and Cornwall, much of life revolves around the pub. Whether you're a banker, a gardener or a student: you'll find all sorts of people rubbing shoulders in the pub. After work, you might have a pint (that's to say 0.568 litres of beer) with your colleagues – but some people come on their own and sit at the bar, then dive into some conversation or other within a few minutes. Pubs aren't just watering holes, they're the places where British society unites, in good times and in bad. There are certain unwritten rules you need to follow:

A taste of the sea:
fish and chips is the way to go

you order at the bar and pay then and there. You don't need to tip in the pub (although sometimes there'll be a tip jar on the bar). Pints are poured right to the brim, so inexperienced drinkers will definitely spill some on their way to the table. This is because there were traditionally no measurement marks on glasses in the UK, and the glass itself acted as the measure: it's only a full pint if it's almost overflowing. This tradition has survived to this day.

ROUND & ROUND

Some of the country roads in Devon and Cornwall are narrow and full of roundabouts. On top of that, everyone drives on what most of the world would consider to be the "wrong" side of the road. But is it really wrong? Designs on old coins suggest that the Romans also rode their horses on the left. The UK is also the odd one out in Europe when it comes to measurements: distances are measured in miles and speed limits are shown in miles per hour. However, shorter measurements tend to be in metres not yards these days.

REGIONAL STYLE

Country-house fashion with a Barbour jacket and herringbone sports coat? That's so yesterday! In Devon and Cornwall popular fashion labels have developed and fashion items now fill the wardrobes of school pupils and students up and down the country. *Jack Wills* from Salcombe in Devon offers understated, high-quality college fashion to rival trendy American labels like Abercrombie & Fitch or Gap. *Saltrock*, founded in Penzance, is a surfer label with sportswear that is similar to the popular brands Quiksilver or Element. *Seasalt* originates from Falmouth in Cornwall and produces modern, summery women's fashion collections. These labels have retail stores in every large town in southwest England.

FISH IS ON THE MENU

It's hardly surprising that fishing is still a way of life on the southwest coast of England. British fishermen bring in about 600,000 tonnes of fish every year. This is significantly less than major competitors in Asia and elsewhere, but enough to supply the island's restaurants and markets with great-tasting, excellent-quality fish and seafood. The ever-popular fish and chips is not your only option. You should also sample more exotic seafood like scallops or oysters, which are frequently on the menu and at reasonable prices.

WANNA BET?

In Britain it feels as if there's a betting shop on every corner, and you can place a bet on virtually any outcome: the first goal of the World Cup, the last goal of the European Championship, the name of the next royal baby, or simply the weather at the start of the holidays – there's always something. The stakes can be low and the payout high, but you're more likely to win nothing at all. Ultimately, the biggest winner is the betting shop. There is a long tradition of greyhound racing and especially horse racing. Racehorses pound the tracks all year round in Devon, with racecourses in Exeter and Newton Abbot. Newsagents sell the magazine *Racing Post*, which is exclusively dedicated to the sport.

HISTORY SET IN STONE

Everybody has heard of Stonehenge, but did you know that stone circles also exist in Devon and Cornwall? Experts assume that natural resources such as tin and copper attracted people here during the Neolithic period. Apparently, our early ancestors transported stones from one end of the island to the other in order to create fascinating stone circles. The function of these circles is still the subject of debate, but the experts ultimately conclude that their purpose was probably religious.

Relics from prehistoric times provide some intriguing names for visitor

TRUE OR FALSE?

CORNWALL & PILCHER

Most people will look blank if you mention the name Rosamunde Pilcher. While she is a household name in much of Europe, she is largely unknown in her home county. Even in Lelant, the little village in west Cornwall where Pilcher was born in 1924, hardly anyone remembers her. This could have something to do with the content of her work. Most people in Cornwall (one of the poorest regions in England) cannot relate to the aristocratic families and magnificent manor houses of her romantic novels.

NOTHING BUT TEA

Do the English drink nothing but tea? Not by a long shot – in recent years, coffee shops have opened up in the furthest reaches of the country, including Cornwall, and most of them serve almost as good a cappuccino as anywhere in Italy. But the Brits, who consume 1.94kg of tea per person per year, still rank in the world's top three tea drinkers, after Turkey and Ireland.

attractions: the *Hurlers Stone Circles*, north of Liskeard, are said to be named after a group who played hurling (a type of rugby) illegally on a Friday and were therefore transformed to stone; the *Merry Maidens*, south of Penzance, is a stone circle dated to the late Stone Age (about 3,000 to 4,000 years ago), and said to depict a group of 19 girls. According to the legend, a spell was cast on them and they were transformed to stone because they performed a dance here on he Sabbath. Have no fear: you will not be subject to these kinds of sanctions today!

MIF OR TIF?

England is a great nation of tea drinkers, and Devon and Cornwall are no exception. The most delicious mealtimes include the little word tea – *high tea, afternoon tea* and – especially in Devon and Cornwall – the ubiquitous *cream tea* (tea and a scone with jam and clotted cream). Breakfast blends from Assam, Ceylon and Kenya are the most popular varieties, and every self-respecting tea drinker will order an Earl Grey, which is supposedly served in royal circles.

What is the correct way to drink tea? The truth is, opinions are divided between *MIF* and *TIF*. While some prefer to pour milk into the cup first (*milk in first* – MIF), others begin with the tea and then add a drop of milk (*tea in first* – TIF). There are pros and cons on both sides, but personal preference is what counts. One thing is for certain: the clotted cream goes on the scone, not in the tea.

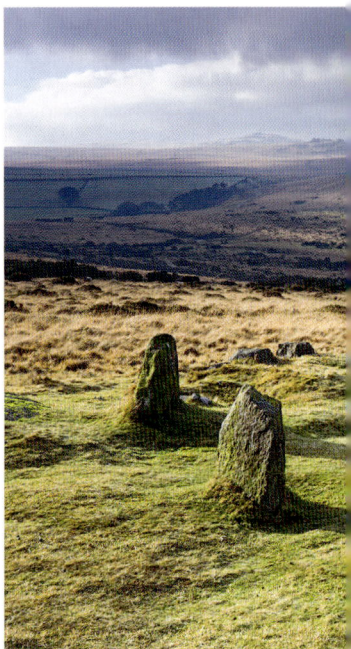

LEGENDARY KING

Almost everybody has heard about the legends surrounding the legendary monarch, King Arthur. Tintagel Castle, on the north Cornish coast, is said to be the site of Arthur's conception, and he supposedly lived in many other places, or was seen or rode past them. Not a single piece of evidence confirms that Arthur ever existed or that his knights ever found the Holy Grail, as it is alleged. What is certain is that the present-day ruins of Tintagel Castle didn't exist during Arthur's "lifetime". Moreover, the many proudly exhibited round tables – around which his knights are said to have congregated – also date to a much later period. It is equally uncertain

Ancient stone circles often have romantic names: the Nine Maidens on Dartmoor

whether the area around Glastonbury in the neighbouring county of Somerset could be the mythical Avalon where King Arthur is said to be buried. Are his mortal remains buried anywhere? The great thing about legends is that they leave so many things open to interpretation.

CHONS DA!

Dydh da, dyw genes, meur ras? If you think that looks like Welsh, think again. These words come from the Cornish language, and they mean "hello", "goodbye" and "thank you". Go into any pub in Ireland and you may hear some Irish Gaelic, and Welsh is hard to miss in Wales, but Cornish struggled for centuries.

Cornish was so far gone that it was considered extinct. But attempts by previous governments to revive the language had some success. Granted, you won't hear it in the street, but the language is starting to be taught in schools in Cornwall again. Plus, the local government has instructed its staff to use as many Cornish words as possible when communicating with the public. Will it make any difference? Well, we can only wish them *chons da* – good luck!

EATING
SHOPPING
SPORT

Wander where smugglers once roamed – in Polperro

EATING & DRINKING

If you are a fan of fish and seafood, then you will love Devon and Cornwall! Cod, lobster, oysters and mussels – seafood served here is generally locally caught and was probably still alive last night. You can taste the freshness.

HEALTHY IS TRENDY

Fortunately, it's a long time since the bars and restaurants mostly served nothing but fish and chips. Famous TV chefs, like Jamie Oliver and Cornwall's masterchef, Rick Stein, have successfully campaigned for healthy eating. They've also set an example: these days chefs in many small country pubs prepare fresh, fine quality food, even in the most remote locations.

WHERE THE COWS ROAM FREE

There is a wide choice, and meat-eaters have plenty of options. Devon and Cornwall are well known for beef and lamb dishes, as the meat is invariably sourced from local farms where the livestock can graze outdoors all year round. This also means the dairy produce is exceptional. While lactose-free and soya-based products are widely available, people here generally love whole milk from English cows. So, the ice cream and yoghurt tends to be creamier in Devon and Cornwall than anywhere else. In the better restaurants, they often use lightly salted butter, as they do in France. And that's not the only similarity: you should have wine, bread and water with your meal. Certain pleasant dining customs have made their way over from the continent.

CHAINS GALORE

There is another popular dish on the food scene: hamburgers. Fast-food chains once dominated the market. In recent years, though, more and more

Both traditional and delicious: cider (left) and scones (right)

trendy chain restaurants, like Byron and Gourmet Burger Kitchen, have opened, selling so-called posh burgers. This reflects another British gastro-food trend: both independent and countrywide restaurant chains have opened here for almost every type of food. The same applies to pubs that are owned by breweries and pub groups, although it is not always obvious from the outside. Local, independent landlords are becoming few and far between.

Traditionally, pubs only served food at lunchtime – but this has changed. More and more pubs offer an extensive dinner menu. Restaurants are usually open from noon to 2.30pm, and from 6.30pm to 9.30pm (last orders). Small restaurants also often close on Mondays.

THE PERFECT DESTINATION FOR VEGGIES & VEGANS

Fitness and healthy eating are very much on trend these days, and most menus have plenty of options for vegetarians and vegans and can usually cater for special dietary requirements. Most menus label the ingredients and friendly advice is offered everywhere if, for example, you need gluten- or lactose-free food or to avoid nuts.

You can save money by buying food in the supermarket or finding a good delicatessen: chains such as Waitrose and Marks & Spencer specialise in high-quality groceries and now have a network of smaller stores selling mainly salads, sandwiches, sushi and fruit selections.

INSIDER TIP
For big appetites

Feast nights are new mass events centred around one thing – food. Everyone brings their

27

own plates, wine and cutlery and gets together for organised dining events. It all takes place outdoors, and it's all very relaxed. The only thing that's taken seriously is the quality of the food. These events are mainly provided by farms.

A PINT DOWN THE PUB

The English love to drink in pubs. Although wine is widely available, beer is still a popular drink. A pub will rarely offer fewer than half a dozen different draught beer varieties; larger pubs may offer twice as many. Lager is a firm favourite; international brands like Heineken or Kronenbourg 1664 are popular, although local breweries also feature frequently: St Austell Brewery's Korev lager holds its own against major competitors. St Ives Brewery also produces a lager, as well as Bays from Paignton in Devon.

The popularity of lagers might have suppressed an original British speciality – real ale, a reddish beer that lacks carbonation. But in the late 1990s, the Campaign for Real Ale (CAMRA) came to the rescue, persuading pub chains to serve more real ale. The beer is drawn at cellar temperature and has become a stalwart choice in pubs. The trend for craft beer has meant that the smaller breweries can also get a look in. As for stout, the dark, velvety, soft beer, Irish Guinness is still the undisputed Number One. However, there too you'll find surprising novelties from local breweries. Have a taste!

A GLASS OF APPLES

Another, much fruitier speciality – cider – is mostly made in the neighbouring counties of Somerset and Dorset. This pleasant-tasting apple beverage contains the same amount of alcohol in Britain as a beer. Numerous varieties are available and, if you venture beyond the usual pub brands, you will find some incredibly creative ciders – some are drier, while others are sweeter than usual, and they can also be made with entirely different fruits.

Today's specials

Starters

OYSTERS
Served with lemon

LEEK AND POTATO SOUP
Hot, creamy soup, perfect for a cold day

CORNISH PILCHARDS
Fried sardines served with bread

CORNISH MUSSELS
Steamed in cider and cream broth

Mains

STARGAZY PIE
Pie made from potatoes and eggs with whole sardines peeping out

CHICKEN TIKKA MASALA
Chicken pieces in a red curry sauce

FISH & CHIPS
Fried, battered fish with chips and, if you like, mushy peas

SUNDAY ROAST
Roast beef with potatoes, vegetables and Yorkshire pudding

COTTAGE PIE
Pie made with minced beef and covered with a layer of mashed potatoes

Desserts

RHUBARB CRUMBLE
Fruit compote baked with a crumble topping, often served with vanilla custard

STICKY TOFFEE PUDDING
Sponge cake covered with date and toffee sauce, often served with vanilla custard

CHEESE BOARD
Cheese platter with cheddar, stilton and other cheeses

Snacks

CORNISH PASTY
Pastry filled with meat and vegetables

JACKET POTATO WITH CHEESE
Baked potato, filled with grated cheddar cheese

CRAB SANDWICH
A sandwich filled with crab meat and mayonnaise

In the afternoon

CREAM TEA
Tea and scones with jam and clotted cream

SHOPPING

ANTIQUES

In southwest England you can acquire plenty of vintage items. Honiton in East Devon is the main centre for antique hunters – there are about two dozen antique shops. Barnstaple is another good place, as well as Lostwithiel, near St Austell in Cornwall. You can buy crockery, glass and much more at the many flea markets dotted around Devon.

FLOWER POWER

There are gardens all over the southwest and they all need to be tended. And that's why there are so many garden centres offering everything from trowels to flowerpots. The National Trust also has shops at its visitor attractions.

ART & CRAFTS

Talented artists are not only found in St Ives; many small towns have privately run galleries which showcase works by local artists. Oils and watercolours with coastal motifs are readily available – these paintings tend to catch the eye of visitors in holiday mood. However, souvenirs also come in different forms: coasters, tea towels, mugs and the like decorated with artistic designs.

BON APPETIT!

Regional food products are particularly important in Devon and Cornwall and, as well as the ubiquitous supermarkets, it is worth checking out the numerous small delicatessens. These often sell home-made jam, sauces, chutneys and much more, made using local ingredients. The *Cornish Sea Salt Company* produces salt from the Lizard Peninsula. Furthermore, approximately 100 different cheese varieties are produced in Devon and Cornwall.

Good choice: a teapot (left) to take home, strawberries (right) to eat right now

PICK-ME-UP & A NIGHTCAP

English tea is internationally famous, although the tea isn't usually English at all, but is sourced from Asia, notably from India and Nepal. However, the *Tregothnan Estate* produces truly English tea, which is grown near Truro. It is sold on site (St Michael Penkivel, Truro), and in selected shops and cafés. Coffee isn't grown in England (yet) but there are some excellent coffee roasteries in the southwest, including *DJ Miles* in Porlock (Exmoor).

If you are looking for a bottle of wine as a souvenir, several wine-growing estates have opened in recent decades. These include *Eastcott*, near Okehampton, and Polgoon, near Penzance. Many of them also produce cider. Gin distilleries are popular as well. In addition to classic *Plymouth Gin*, there are numerous smaller producers, such as *Elemental* from St Columb.

INSIDER TIP
Tea for two

RIDE THE WAVES IN STYLE

Leave your bathing suit at home and buy what you need when you arrive. Swimming and surfwear is widely available in coastal resorts, especially Newquay. Many items are not necessarily cheaper here, but the choice is wide. *Saltrock* and *Finisterre* are two cool surfwear brands from Cornwall – for anyone looking to buck the well-known international trends.

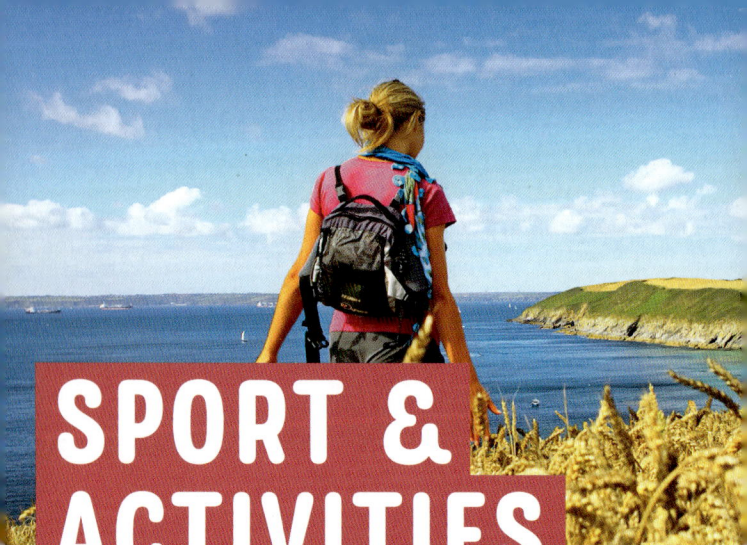

SPORT & ACTIVITIES

The craze for jogging and fitness has long since reached the south-west of England – fitness studios have sprung up everywhere and every morning you will notice cheery people out for a run on the beach.

Cycling is popular too. In Devon and Cornwall, surfing is a traditional sport and swimming in the sea is so convenient that many people have taken to swimming year-round. Tennis and golf are national sports – expensive club memberships are no longer required to enjoy these activities.

COASTEERING

This adventure sport basically involves exploring rocky cliffs, climbing the rocks, jumping off them into the sea, swimming into small caves and making the ascent again – a bit mad, but really cool. This fun but potentially dangerous sport should only be tried in organised groups (£35 to £50 per person). You can have a go in plenty of coastal resorts, including Land's End, Salcombe and on the Isles of Scilly. *Information: britishcoasteering federation.org*

CYCLING

Today, the UK cycle network covers over 20,000km and there are many routes in Devon and Cornwall that often head through amazing countryside; try, for example, the *Camel Trail* near Padstow or the *Granite Way* near Lydford. If you're feeling fit, you can tackle *Route 27,* between Ilfracombe and Plymouth. It connects North Devon and South Devon across 159km, and traverses moorland and Victorian viaducts as well as passing stunning beaches and estuaries. You'll find a cycle-hire shop in most tourist

INSIDER TIP
Full wheel ahead!

Simply glorious: walk along the South West Coast Path

resorts (approx. £20 per day). *Information: sustrans.org.uk*

DIVING

The coastline is dotted with thousands of shipwrecks. There are about 3,500 of them off the Cornish coast alone. The bad weather, conflicts and reefs have made their mark over the centuries. While this is bad news for shipping, it offers plenty of adventures for divers. Despite the often-cold water, diving remains a popular sport here. The Isles of Scilly are another popular diving area – about 1,000 shipwrecks are located here, and between Bude and Hartland there is a similar number. *Information about the best diving locations: bsac.com*

FISHING

You can fish for trout and sometimes even salmon in the lakes and rivers of Devon and Cornwall. To cast a line you will need a rod licence that can be issued by angling clubs and post offices (from £5 per day depending on the type of fish).

The South West Lakes Trust *(swlakesfishing.co.uk)* maintains a number of lakes and issues licences for them too. No licence is required for sea fishing. In many ports, special half-day and day tours are available for keen anglers. *Information: anglingtrust.net*

HIKING

The southwest is a paradise for hikers. There is, of course, the *South West Coast Path (southwestcoastpath.org.uk)*, that runs for 1,014km from Minehead in Somerset, along the coasts of Devon and Cornwall, to Poole Harbour in Dorset. And there are also numerous smaller signposted routes, particularly on Exmoor and Dartmoor. During the winter you should pack sufficient supplies, as the coastal cafés and kiosks will generally be closed. You can join organised hiking tours almost everywhere; contact the local tourist information offices for more details. You are unlikely to encounter any danger – except (very rare) adders and (more often) cows that should be given a wide berth. And don't underestimate the weather: coastal paths are beautiful, but you should avoid them in very strong winds, and under no circumstances should you venture along them during storms. Often, the paths stretch for miles without anywhere to divert off from them. There may be powerful gusts of wind, and thunder and lightning can be life-threatening. The BBC's weather reports are fairly reliable, as is the free app from the official Met Office.

A paper map or offline map could be useful, as you can't always get a phone signal along the coast.

RIDING

On Exmoor and Dartmoor ponies are very much a part of the scenery; indeed Exmoor ponies are well known across England and beyond. Several hotels and B&Bs offer riding holidays, and you can also join in short riding tours here. In the UK, paths that are suitable for horses are called bridleways *(bhsaccess.org.uk/ridemaps)*. *Information: bhs.org.uk | visitexmoor. co.uk/horse-riding*

SAILING

Most traditional sailing venues are along the south coast, generally towards Hampshire and Sussex. But South Devon and Cornwall are also popular with many sailors. Fowey and Dartmouth are classic sailing centres, as are the Isles of Scilly. The main regattas are the *Torbay Royal Regatta, Falmouth Week Regatta* and the *Port of Dartmouth Royal Regatta* (all during August). *Information: rya.org.uk*

STAND-UP PADDLE BOARDING

Surfing has long been a part of Cornish identity. However, recently some people also like to take their paddleboards with them – and fall into the water sooner or later. You can now learn stand-up paddle boarding in almost all major surfing centres in southwest England. You can also hire wetsuits and equipment. *Information: bsupa.org.uk.*

Boards ahoy – surfers will enjoy the miles of beach in Cornwall

SURFING

Newquay is one of the top surfing centres in Europe thanks to its long beaches and fabulous surf conditions. Sennen Cove in Cornwall and Bigbury in Devon are also popular with surfers. Almost all major beaches offer surf boards and wetsuits for hire (about £10) as well as courses for all abilities (from £30). *Information: surfing england.org | surfing-cornwall.com*

TENNIS

Of course, Wimbledon has made sure that tennis never goes out of fashion in the UK. Many larger hotels have tennis courts. The campaign *Tennis for Free (tennisforfree.com)* aims to provide as many tennis courts and courses as possible free of charge. There are four courses so far in Devon and Cornwall (Plymouth, Truro and two in Exeter). *Information: tennishub. co.uk*

WAKEBOARDING

Waterskiing is so yesterday! Strap yourself onto a wakeboard and allow the boat to skim you along the water. A bit of adrenalin, plenty of beautiful nature – and you're guaranteed to get wet in the end. This sport is perfect for water-loving Cornwall. You can try it out in Penryn at *Kernow Adventure Park (kernowadventurepark.com)* and in Padstow at *Camel Ski School (camelskischool.com).*

REGIONAL OVERVIEW

CELTIC SEA

EAST CORNWALL p. 60

Bodmin

WEST CORNWALL p. 38

St Austell

Penzance

Heavenly England: pristine beaches, clear water and idyllic villages

Cliffs and ponies: unspoilt Devon landscape

NORTH DEVON p. 98

Bristol Channel

Barnstaple

Torridge

Taw

Exe

Exeter

SOUTH DEVON p. 76

Colliford Lake

Torquay

Plymouth

Something for everyone: hiking, partying, relaxing

Wild and rugged: history, ports and plenty of myths and legends

English Channel

20 km
12.43 mi

WEST CORNWALL

ENGLAND'S HEAVENLY CORNER

It takes almost six hours to drive from London to West Cornwall – but that doesn't stop everyone from wanting to visit England's corner of heaven. With its pristine beaches, clear waters and smattering of little villages, the place will make you feel as if the capital city is light years away.

Britain's westernmost point, Land's End, is here, as is its most southerly tip at Lizard Point. The landscape looks like a film set – and indeed the scenery has been the backdrop for numerous movies

All your beach dreams come true at Bedruthan Steps, near Newquay

and television series. In the southwest, you will meet rugged and eccentric characters whose livelihoods are centred outside Britain's metropolitan areas. You will also come across well-travelled people who have brought back food trends from France, surfer fashion from Australia and technology from Tokyo, and have shared their findings by setting up new hotels, restaurants and beach shops. In parts of West Cornwall you might feel as if time has stood still – but the place is very cool in its own way.

WEST CORNWALL

MARCO POLO HIGHLIGHTS

★ **EDEN PROJECT**
Magnificent domes: the climates of the world can be experienced at this former clay quarry. ➤ p. 42

★ **LIZARD POINT**
Cornwall's best view and a beautiful lighthouse await on the Lizard Peninsula – the perfect place to get lost. ➤ p. 47

★ **ST MICHAEL'S MOUNT**
High tide, low tide and a tiny island: England's castle in the sea is almost as impressive as its French counterpart, Mont-Saint-Michel. ➤ p. 50

★ **MINACK THEATRE**
Unique open-air theatre in a rocky clifftop setting. ➤ p. 51

★ **ISLES OF SCILLY**
This remote group of islands has abundant beaches, flowers – and sunshine. ➤ p. 53

★ **TATE ST IVES**
London's Tate Gallery on the beach in Cornwall exhibits leading artworks, and includes a fabulous sea view. ➤ p. 56

★ **NEWQUAY BEACHES**
One bay after another and endless surfing fun. ➤ p. 58

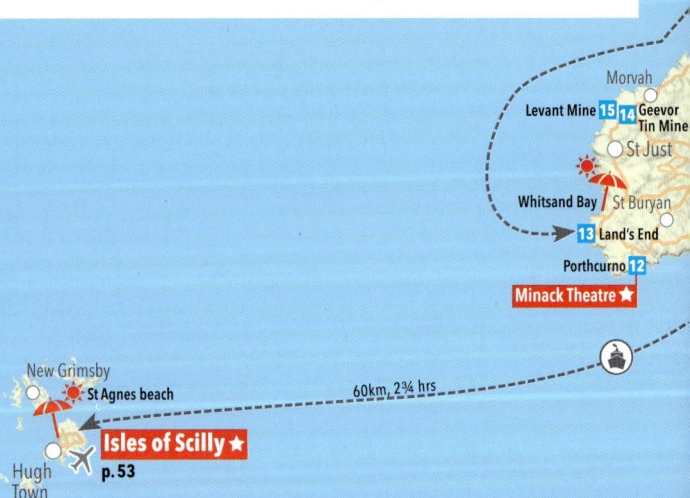

Morvah

Levant Mine 15 14 Geevor Tin Mine

St Just

Whitsand Bay   St Buryan

13 Land's End

Porthcurno 12

Minack Theatre ★

New Grimsby

St Agnes beach

60km, 2¾ hrs

Isles of Scilly ★
p. 53

Hugh Town

10 km
6.21 mi

CELTIC SEA

Tintagel

Port Isaac

Polzeath

St Kew Highway

Padstow

Wadebridge

39

Mount Charles

18 Bedruthan Steps

CORNWALL

Watergate Bay
6km,
1½ hrs

St Columb Major

30

Newquay beaches ★

Newquay
p. 57

Roche

Stenalees

Holywell

16 Trerice

Eden Project ★ **1**

Lappa Valley
Steam Railway

17

p. 42
St Austell

Perranporth

30

6 St Agnes Heritage Coast

5 Healeys Cornish Cyder Farm

Grampound

68km, 1 hr 10 mins

Lost Gardens of Heligan **2**

Mevagissey **3**

Porthtowan Beach

39

Portreath

390

Truro
p. 43

Tregony

Tate St Ives ★

43km, 45 mins

Redruth

4 Trelissick Garden

Gorran Haven

Porthmeor Beach

Camborne

Ponsanooth

7 Roseland

St Ives
p. 55

30

Praze-An-Beeble

Penryn

Gerrans

Hayle

Falmouth
p. 45

Leedstown

Poldark
Mine

Gyllyngvase Beach

Penzance
p. 49

10 Godolphin

9

394

Marazion

Helston

Mawnan Smith

11

St Michael's Mount ★

46km, 50 mins

St Keverne

8 Porthleven

Mullion

Lizard
p. 47

Coverack

Lizard Point ★

English Channel

ST AUSTELL

(□ G9) **It may come as a surprise to discover that St Austell (pop. 34,700) is Cornwall's biggest town: the town centre seems rather small and the major visitor attractions have emerged relatively recently.**

St Austell was for many centuries a centre for the kaolin (china clay) industry. Tourism has only flourished since the 1990s, when the last clay pits closed in the southwest. You can find out more about the history at the *Wheal Martyn China Clay Heritage Centre (daily 10am–4pm | admission adults £15, children (5–15) £7 | Wheal Martyn | Carthew | wheal-martyn.com | 5km north of the town centre).*

SIGHTSEEING

ST AUSTELL BREWERY ☂

You can see how some of Cornwall's best-known beers are produced here. St Austell Brewery produces various lagers, ales and stouts. *Mon–Sat 9am–5pm | tours (11am and 2pm) £20, tasting session £12.50 | 63 Trevarthian Road | staustellbrewery visitorcentre.co.uk | ⊙ 2 hrs*

CHARLESTOWN

At the end of the 19th century, it was important to find a harbour to ship out the kaolin. St Austell developed this port from a small fishing village. Cargo ships no longer dock here; this once-small village is better known today for its role as a backdrop in the filming of the television series *Poldark*.

The *Shipwreck and Heritage Centre (March–Oct daily 10am–5pm | admission £5.95 | Quay Road | shipwreck charlestown.com | ⊙ 1 hr)* presents exhibitions about the numerous shipwrecks just off the coast. The centre professes to possess the largest collection of its kind in Europe.

EATING & DRINKING

THE LONGSTORE

Steaks and fish are what attract people to this restaurant in Charlestown with a view over the harbour. The atmosphere is casual and modern, the food classic and sophisticated. *Harbour Front | tel. 01726 68598 | thelongstore. co.uk | £££*

AROUND ST AUSTELL

1 EDEN PROJECT ★ ☂

5km / 10 mins northeast of St Austell (by car)

In the James Bond film *Die Another Day* the hero crosses these vast plastic domes. Like a spaceship, they span parts of a former kaolin pit and are the heart of an ambitious project whereby the world's climatic zones are recreated beneath domes or "biomes". Plants from all over the world grow here. The air humidity and temperatures are tropical in places. The energy is mainly generated by wind and solar farms. On the edge of the site is an unusual *youth hostel (16 rooms | tel. 0345 371*

9573 (*) | yha.org.uk), which offers glamping, and you can sleep in Airstream caravans and top-of-the-range tents. *Daily 9.30am–6pm, in winter 9.30am–4pm | admission £32.50 (online booking required) | Bodelva, Par | edenproject. com | ⏱ 3–4 hrs | 🗺 G9*

2 LOST GARDENS OF HELIGAN 🚩

10km / 15 mins south of St Austell (by car)

The lost gardens are blooming once again: they were cultivated back in the 18th century but later were abandoned and became overgrown. That was until the initiator of the Eden Project, Tim Smit, discovered and restored them to their former glory. The site comprises several gardens with different designs. Even pineapples grow in the Victorian Productive Gardens! *Daily April–Oct 10am–6pm, Nov–March 10am–5pm | admission £18.50 | Pentewan | heligan.com | ⏱ 2–3 hrs | 🗺 G9*

3 MEVAGISSEY

10km / 12 mins south of St Austell (by car)

A picturesque fishing village (pop. 2,000): boats are moored in the harbour, and on both sides of it are narrow streets running uphill, lined with small cottages. It comes as no surprise that the village is well known for its tasty fish dishes, for example at *Sharksfin (The Quay | tel. 01726 842969 | thesharksfin.co.uk | ££)* in the harbour. From May to September a small ferry travels several times a day from Mevagissey to Fowey, with a superb view of the coastline.

TRURO

(🗺 E9–10) **The only genuine capital of Cornwall is Truro (pop. 19,000).**

The town centre, between Lemon Street and Victoria Square, offers something for all shoppers and if you fancy something to eat or drink, you've come to the right place. The centre is packed with pubs and restaurants offering a wide selection. Truro, which became Cornwall's capital in the 19th century, was once labelled "Cornwall's London" because of its many impressive Georgian and

A picture-book fishing village: Mevagissey

Victorian buildings. Nowadays it is more modest, but the town is well worth visiting, not only for its strategic central location.

SIGHTSEEING

TRURO CATHEDRAL

Although the Gothic Revival cathedral appears very old, it was in fact only finished in 1910, earning Truro the title of "city" (because a city needs a cathedral) – a befitting title for the capital of Cornwall. You can enjoy beautiful choral music on weekdays from 5.30pm at ✝ *Choral Evensong.* On the south side of the cathedral are the remains of St Mary's Church that made way for the new building. *Mon–Sat 10am–5pm, Sun 11.30am–4.30pm | free admission | 14 St Mary's Street | trurocathedral.org.uk | ⏱ 30 mins*

ROYAL CORNWALL MUSEUM ✝

In Cornwall's oldest museum you can find out about the county's history and enter a treasure trove of archaeology, antiquities and artworks. They also have an ambitious programme of temporary exhibitions and events. *Tue–Sat 10am–4pm | admission £7.50 (under 18s free) | River Street | royalcornwallmuseum.org.uk | ⏱ 1 hr*

EATING & DRINKING

BUSTOPHER JONES

This chic bistro looks more like a bright, seaside pub. But the most important thing is that you can eat well here: the fish and meat dishes are delicious and there are also vegetarian options. How about asparagus crêpes, duck breast or a whole lobster? *62 Lemon Street | tel. 01872 430000 | bustopher-jones. co.uk | £££*

THE CORNISH VEGAN

A vegan restaurant in a central location with fabulous creations, including a vegan take on fish and chips, a buddha bowl

INSIDER TIP
Nothing fishy here!

and vegan nuggets, which strongly resemble the chicken version. *15 Kenwyn Street | tel. 01872 271540 | thecornishvegan.com | ££*

Lofty Truro Cathedral

AROUND TRURO

4 TRELISSICK GARDEN

8km / 12 mins south of Truro (by car)

The estate on the peninsula in the Fal river estuary offers 12 hectares of countryside with panoramic views. Gingko, rhododendron, camellia and many more species grow here thanks to the mild climate. Images of these plants were beautifully hand painted on the porcelain that the Copeland family, the former owners of Trelissick, produced in their factory. Their magnificent country house is also open to visitors. *Daily 10am–5pm (March–Oct house and garden, Nov–Feb garden only) | admission £13, parking £5 | Feock | nationaltrust.org.uk/trelissick | ⏱ 2 hrs | ▥ E10*

5 HEALEYS CORNISH CYDER FARM

10km / 15 mins northwest of Truro (by car)

Cider is as much a part of Devon and Cornwall as cream teas and pasties. The carbonated apple drink is available in every pub. Healeys Cornish Cyder Farm produces the alcoholic beverage and provides a great overview of how it's made. You can sample the farm's produce with a tasting at the end. Guided tours, including by tractor, start from £5. *Daily 9am–5pm | admission from £8 | Penhallow, Truro | thecornishcyderfarm.co.uk | ⏱ 1 hr | ▥ E9*

6 ST AGNES HERITAGE COAST

14km / 18 mins northwest of Truro (via the A390/B3277)

The pretty, rather sleepy village of St Agnes lends its name to this whole stretch of coast in the north of Cornwall. Here, you will encounter cliffs and rugged fields, centuries-old pubs and plenty of hiking routes. The old pump house at *Wheal Coates (always open | free admission | Beacon Drive, St Agnes | nationaltrust.org.uk/wheal-coates)* stands like a memorial on the coast. Only the walls and a chimney remain, but it makes a fabulous subject for photographs, especially at sunrise or sunset. Wheal Coates dates back to the latter half of the 19th century, when tin mining was the main source of income in the region. Just 100 years later, all the mines in Cornwall gradually closed. ▥ D9

FALMOUTH

(▥ E10–11) **Life in Falmouth (pop. 20,000) has always revolved around the deep natural harbour on the Fal Estuary.**

From here ferries make the crossing to St Mawes. You can find out more about maritime history in the National Maritime Museum. The town centre also has quaint narrow alleys and Georgian houses. A number of beautiful beaches on the outskirts of Falmouth attract crowds during the summer.

Bring your nets: exciting discoveries on Falmouth beach

SIGHTSEEING

NATIONAL MARITIME MUSEUM

This regional branch of London's National Maritime Museum has a full-scale replica of a Viking ship for visitors to enjoy along with underwater exploration and exciting reports from fishermen of bygone days. The view from the lookout tower offers sweeping views across the harbour. Seafaring was an important part of the Cornish way of life for centuries – and here you will find out why. *Daily 10am–5pm | admission adults £18, under 18s £9, under 5s free | Discovery Quay | nmmc.co.uk |* ⏱ *2 hrs*

PENDENNIS CASTLE

Four hundred and fifty years of history: the old fortress on a rocky headland near the harbour is not only striking to look at, but it also has several exhibitions inside; there's one about World War I and another about daily life in Victorian times. *April–Oct daily, Nov–March Sat/Sun 10am–4pm | admission adults £17.20, children £10.40 (cheaper if booked online in advance) | Castle Drive | english-heritage.org.uk |* ⏱ *1 hr*

EATING & DRINKING

FOUR

This restaurant in the centre of Falmouth may not have the biggest selection, but the dishes are delicious and very varied. There is a range of fish and meat, and most can easily compete with gourmet places in London or other major cities. *33 High Street | tel. 01326 218138 | restaurantfour.co.uk | ££*

BEACHES

Right in town, 🐾 *Gyllyngvase Beach* is a lovely, reasonably sized sandy beach with a view over the crystal-clear water. Further west, *Swanpool Beach* is calmer but not quite as nice.

AROUND FALMOUTH

🔟 ROSELAND

10 mins from Falmouth (by ferry)
On the other side of Carrick Roads harbour is the Roseland peninsula,

with the sleepy fishing village of St Mawes (pop. 850), which resembles a smaller version of Falmouth. A network of alleyways criss-crosses the village, which also has a fort: *St Mawes Castle (April–Oct daily, Nov–March Sat/Sun 10am–4pm | admission £11.80, children £7.20 (cheaper if booked online in advance) | Castle Drive | english-heritage.org.uk)*. The Roseland is popular with wildlife enthusiasts, with its green hills and diversity of birds. *St Anthony Lighthouse* here is not only one of England's most attractive lighthouses but also contains a holiday residence where you can stay. ⊞ E10

LIZARD

(⊞ D-E 11–12) **On the Lizard Peninsula the idyllic scenery is perfect for filming romantic novels.**

Rocky clifftops, formed by the waves of the Atlantic Ocean, define this part of Cornwall. Down below you will find the fine sandy beaches, and on the cliffs, vast stretches of grassland, cows, and quaint villages. Make sure you don't just whizz through in your car – get out and enjoy the sights.

SIGHTSEEING

KYNANCE COVE

The greenish-brown serpentine stone in this beautiful bay reflects vibrant red hues at sunset. It is well worth a visit at other times of the day too, and you should preferably walk along the impressive coastal path from Lizard Point (3km away). There is a wonderful view overlooking the bay from *Kynance Café (March–Oct only | Kynance Cove | kynancecovecafe.co.uk | £). nationaltrust.org.uk/kynance-cove*

LIZARD POINT ⭐

Lizard Point is not only England's southernmost tip, but also a magnificent destination for walking and hiking tours, preferably along the coast. The white *Lizard Lighthouse (Lizard Village | May–Oct Mon–Thu 11am–5pm | admission £8.50 | trinityhouse.co.uk)* is visible from afar, and is the only lighthouse in Cornwall where you can still climb all the way to the top. Only a short walk in an easterly direction is Bass Point and the *Lizard Wireless Station (Apr–Sept Mon–Thu noon–3pm | free admission | short. travel/cod14)*, where in 1900, the Italian inventor Guglielmo Marconi undertook groundbreaking wireless experiments. The unassuming yet intriguing site, with wooden cabins, still stands today. One of the cabins has been converted to a simple holiday cottage *(Wireless Cottage | 1 room | tel. 0344 800 2070 (*) | nationaltrustholidays. org.uk/holidays | ££)*.

INSIDER TIP
Holiday in a radio station

ST KEVERNE

Make sure you stop off in this village (pop. 2,100), which is one of the most photogenic on the Lizard Peninsula: the 16th-century church is surrounded by attractive small houses and numerous palm trees. This is also a place of historic interest: in 1497, the Cornish rebellion was started in St Keverne when residents protested against the king's tax increases. However, the uprising was thwarted. A statue commemorates the event. Just outside the village of St Keverne is the farm 🐷 *Roskilly's (Tregellast Barton Farm | School Hill | roskillys. co.uk)*, which is famed for its real Cornish ice cream made from the creamy milk of the Jersey cows they keep here. You can also walk around the grounds for free.

INSIDER TIP
Cornish ice cream

EATING & DRINKING

ANN'S PASTIES

If you only try one *Cornish pasty* in your lifetime – do it in this little shop.

Ann Muller learned the art of pasty-making from her mother and has now perfected it. Her award-winning pasties are famous throughout the country. They come with a variety of fillings. Buy one here, go down to Lizard Point and have a picnic. *Sunny Corner | Beacon Terrace | annspasties.co.uk | £*

POLPEOR CAFÉ

From scones to seafood platters, you can enjoy a whole day here – but the excellent food in this little, admittedly rather touristy, café on Lizard Point isn't the star of the show. Instead, it's the fabulous view you will remember forever. *Lizard Point | £*

Fine sandy beaches beneath rugged cliffs are typical of the Lizard Peninsula

SPORT & ACTIVITIES

FLAMBARDS EXPERIENCE

Fun and entertainment any time: the small theme park near Helston not only offers carousels, go-karts and the Skyraker ride but also parts of the Concorde prototype including the cockpit. *April–Oct daily 10am–5pm, Nov–March (only indoors) Tue–Thu 10am–4pm | admission £21.95, only indoor attraction £9.95 | Clodgey Lane, Helston | flambards.co.uk*

AROUND LIZARD

8 PORTHLEVEN

22km / 30 mins northwest of Lizard Point (via the A3083)

The small fishing port (pop. 3,000) near Helston is a popular spot for photographers waiting for extreme waves. In autumn and winter in particular, the water often lashes against the coast in waves that reach several metres high. But Porthleven is worth visiting at other times too. There are some little shops and cafés by the harbour, including *Amélie (Mount Pleasant Road | tel. 01326 653653 | ameliesporthleven.co.uk | ££),* serving Cornish mussels and rosemary potatoes. Fancy a walk? In the southeast is *Penrose (nationaltrust.org.uk/penrose),* a picturesque stretch of countryside by *The Loe,* Cornwall's largest natural freshwater lake.

9 POLDARK MINE

25km / 25 mins north of Lizard Point (via the A3083)

Poldark Mine is Cornwall's only underground tin mine that is still open to visitors today. If you take a tour of the mine, you will see how exhausting life underground must have been. *April–Oct daily, Nov–March Tue, Thu, Sat 10.30am–3pm | admission museum £7 with tour £20 or £27 | Trenear, Wendron | poldarkmine.org.uk | ⏱ 2 hrs | ▥ D11*

10 GODOLPHIN

20km / 30 mins north of Lizard Point (by car)

This house and country estate dates to Tudor times and looks like a castle that was built rather too flat, with its imposing stone façade and rectangular battlements. Mining was still carried out here until well into the 20th century. You can follow the paths through the beautiful medieval gardens. At the southwestern end, there is a fantastic view as far as St Ives Bay and the tidal island of St Michael's Mount. *Daily Jan–Oct 10am–5pm, Nov/Dec 10am–4pm (house only on specific days June–Oct) | admission £11 | Godolphin Cross | Helston | nationaltrust.org.uk/godolphin | ⏱ 1½ hrs | ▥ C11*

PENZANCE

(▥ B11) **The smell of fish and the sea hangs in the air in Penzance (pop. 21,000).**

The town has kept its reputation as a fishing port – more industrious than picturesque. Sardine shoals still run off the coast here, and nearby Newlyn continues to be one of the most important fishing ports in Great Britain. Penzance is something of a hub on this tip of Cornwall. The town will probably never earn accolades as one of Britain's most beautiful, but it has its charms. The main shopping area is Market Jew Street, at the far end of which is a 19th-century *Market Building* with an impressive dome.

SIGHTSEEING

NEWLYN ART GALLERY ☂

It's hard to believe that the small fishing port of Newlyn, now attached to neighbouring Penzance, once attracted artists from around the world. The *Newlyn School of Arts* was a late Impressionist artists' colony. This gallery features several works from that time. You can visit another branch of the gallery at *The Exchange* in Penzance. *Tue–Sat, 10am–5pm, in summer also Mon | admission £7 (for both galleries) | New Road, Newlyn | newlynartgallery.co.uk*

TRENGWAINTON GARDEN

Many of the plants that grow in this garden just outside Penzance shouldn't thrive in the British Isles, including magnolias and camellias. Many of the plants originally came from India and Myanmar. It's a veritable explosion of colour, especially in the summer! *Feb–Oct Sun–Thu 10am–5pm | admission £11 | Madron | national-trust.org.uk/trengwainton-garden | ⏲ 2 hrs*

EATING & DRINKING

MACKEREL SKY SEAFOOD BAR

This ultra-chic little bistro gets freshly caught fish and whisks it straight to your plate. They serve the likes of crab sandwiches, fish fillets or the obligatory sardines. But it's worth the visit even if you're just having a latte. *March–Oct only | The Bridge | New Road | Newlyn | tel. 01736 448982 | mackerelskycafe.co.uk | £*

SPORT & ACTIVITIES

JUBILEE POOL

On the promenade, the Art Deco lido dating from 1935 was refurbished in 2015 and is now a modern leisure pool. The latest additions are a geothermal pool and a café. The place not only features a large seawater pool but also an amazing view of St Michael's Mount and the artists' village of Newlyn. *May–Sept daily 10.30am–6pm | admission £6 | Promenade | jubileepool.co.uk*

AROUND PENZANCE

11 ST MICHAEL'S MOUNT ★

6km / 10 mins east of Penzance (via Long Rock Bypass/A30)

Especially at sunrise and sunset, the tidal island of St Michael's Mount offers romantic views, similar to those at Mont-Saint-Michel over the Channel in France. The similarity is no

St Michael's Mount resembles France's Mont-Saint-Michel, not just in name

accident: in the 11th century, King Edward (the Confessor) gifted the small island to the Benedictine monks from Normandy who built a monastery here. You can walk to St Michael's Mount at low tide, while boats and an amphibious vehicle offer transport at high tide. *March–Oct Sun–Fri 9.30am–5pm, Nov, Dec and Feb Tue, Fri 10.30am–4pm | admission £15, with garden £26 | Marazion | stmichaelsmount.co.uk | ⏱ 2 hrs | 📖 C11*

12 PORTHCURNO

15km / 24 mins southwest of Penzance (by car)

This picturesque location on the coast, with a wonderful sandy beach, owes its development to modern telecommunications. At times, up to 14 cables from the US, India and continental Europe were laid under the sea. *PK Porthcurno (daily April–Oct 10am–5pm, Nov–March 11am–3.30pm | admission £10 | Eastern House | pkporthcurno.com)* provides more information. Here, you can now also view a network of tunnels – a long-kept secret – that were hewn into the rocks in 1941 to protect against invasion. The nearby ⭐ *Minack Theatre (daily March–Sept 9.30am–5pm, Oct–Feb 10am–3.30pm | admission with tour £8 | guided tours in summer, check schedule | Porthcurno Coast | minack.com)* is an impressive place: it was built in 1934 high on the cliffs and is Great Britain's oldest open-air theatre. 📖 B11

INSIDER TIP
Top secret!

The Minack Theatre has to be one of the world's finest open-air theatres

13 LAND'S END ⚑

15km / 22 mins west of Penzance (by car)

England's westernmost landmark relies on its unique selling point. There you'll find the *First and Last Inn* as well as an interactive exhibition mainly designed for children. The tourist attractions are crowded but there is a spectacular rocky coastline. It is well worth exploring the coastal path. Head 4km up the coast and you will come to *Sennen Cove – Whitesand Bay* is one of the most beautiful beaches in Cornwall. *landsend-landmark.co.uk* | 🗺 *A11*

14 GEEVOR TIN MINE

12km / 15 mins northwest of Penzance (via the A3071/B3318)

If you want to delve deeper into Cornwall's mining history, this is the place to do it. At Geevor Tin Mine, you can enter the old tunnels, and the museum will give you loads of insights into life underground. For centuries Devon and Cornwall made their living from mining: tin and copper were extracted here, but also smaller quantities of silver and zinc. It's believed that mines existed here over 4,000 years ago. Geevor Tin Mine produced tin between 1911 and 1990. *Sun–Thu April–Oct 9am–5pm, Nov–March 10am–4pm | mine tours in summer from 10am | admission £17.70 | Penwith Heritage Coast, Pendeen | geevor.com | 🕐 2 hrs |* 🗺 *B10*

🔟 LEVANT MINE

12km / 15 mins northwest of Penzance (via the A3071/B3318)

There is another former mine not far from Geevor. Levant Mine still has a few buildings standing, as well as the ruins of the pumphouse. There is also a 100-year-old steam-powered beam engine, which is brought to life for the benefit of visitors. A serious accident occurred in the mine in 1919, which caused 31 miners to be buried; part of the mine was abandoned at that time. *Sun–Thu summer 10.30am–4.30pm, winter 10.30am–3pm | admission adults £12, children £6 | Trewellard, Pendeen | short.travel/cod16 | ⏱ 1 hr | 🗺 B10*

ISLES OF SCILLY

(🗺 A-B 9–10) **The ⭐ Isles of Scilly are probably the least familiar part of England. This is not the only reason why they are so interesting.**

The Isles of Scilly (pop. 2,200) lie southwest of Land's End and are so remote from the rest of the British Isles that residents have created a world of their own. The water is crystal clear (like that of the South Pacific), the sun shines relatively often and exotic plants grow everywhere. The islands offer everything you need for a relaxing holiday. The only thing missing here is the ordinary hustle and bustle. Travel by plane from Exeter *(March–Oct only)*, Newquay and Land's End *(from £100 each way)*, or by boat from Penzance *(March–Oct | from £78.75 each way)*. There are cheap day trips *(from £35 return)* by boat or plane, or a combination of both.

INSIDER TIP
A day in paradise

SIGHTSEEING

ST MARY'S

The biggest of the Isles of Scilly also has the largest population (1,800 residents). You'll find most essential amenities – such as shops, banks, restaurants and bicycle hire – in the small capital *Hugh Town*. A good starting point are the bus tours run by *Island Rover (Mon–Sat 10.15am and 1.30pm | £10 | Lower Strand | tel. 01720 422131 | islandrover.co.uk)*. The *Boatsmen Association (from £13 return | Rose Cottage, The Strand | tel. 01720 423999 | scillyboating.co.uk)* offers crossings to other islands – you should check the schedule at the harbour, as it changes daily.

ST AGNES

England's last bastion in the Atlantic – in fact St Agnes, not Land's End, is the westernmost point of Great Britain. The white sandy beaches are beautiful and the rugged green countryside is inviting for a short hike. St Agnes is also home to one of England's smallest farms: *Troytown Farm (troytown.co.uk)* produces delicious ice cream, *clotted cream* and butter with milk from nine Jersey cows.

INSIDER TIP
Ice cream on an idyllic island

TRESCO

On the traffic-free island of Tresco, north of St Mary's, you can relax on the beach and forget everyday routines – simply because there's no one else there to bother you. The enchanting *Tresco Abbey Garden (daily 10am–4pm | admission £18 | tresco.co.uk)*, which displays plants from countries all over the world, such as Brazil, New Zealand and South Africa, is bound to render you speechless even if you don't know the first thing about gardening. Equally impressive is the nearby *Valhalla Museum*: the figureheads here give an insight into the treacherous seas around the islands – they all come from sunken ships.

BRYHER

At low tide you can walk from Tresco to this small, rugged island. Bryher offers fabulous opportunities for hiking and snorkelling, as the sea here is calmer than it is near the other islands. And once you've finished exerting yourself, you need not feel guilty about indulging in one of the island's top delicacies: home-made fudge is available from the farm owned by Kris and Geoff Taylor *(Veronica Farm | veronicafarmfudge. co.uk)*.

INSIDER TIP
Indulge your sweet tooth

EATING & DRINKING

FRAGGLE ROCK BAR

You can enjoy views of the picturesque bay through the window, but when the sun is shining, the loveliest spot is right outside the door. This unassuming restaurant serves modern British cuisine prepared with locally sourced produce. Even the wine here comes from Cornwall and almost everything else is locally grown on the Isles of Scilly. *Harbour View, Bryher | tel. 01720 422222 | bryher.co | £*

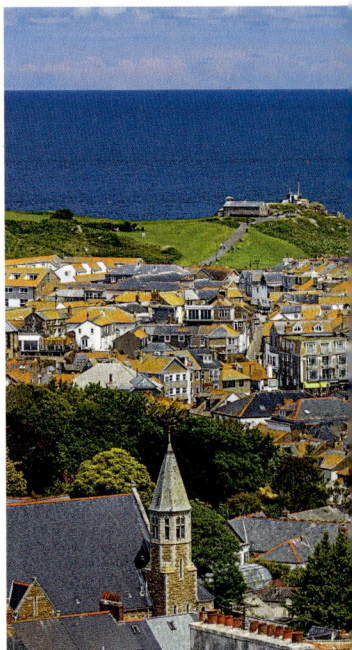

JULIET'S GARDEN

Leave plenty of time for this restaurant a little way outside Hugh Town. You order delicious dishes and light bites here, and the food comes with an incredible view across the bay of Hugh Town. *Seaway, Porthlow, St Mary's | tel. 01720 422228 | julietsgarden restaurant.co.uk | £££*

St Ives, nestled around its harbour, is the perfect spot on a summer's day

SPORT & ACTIVITIES

The Isles of Scilly are the ideal spot for snorkelling and diving, not just because of the crystal-clear water, but also because about 900 shipwrecks are dotted around the islands. You can try *Scilly Seal Snorkelling (£49 | St Martin's | tel. 01720 422848 | scilly sealsnorkelling.com)*. There aren't any mountains, so the hiking routes aren't exactly challenging, but all the islands are certainly beautiful. The fine sandy beaches are also perfect for sunbathing.

ST IVES

(⌑ C10) **In St Ives (pop. 11,000) you just have to get creative: this is Cornwall's artists' centre.**

It also has four beaches that are all picture-postcard perfect with crystal-clear water, cute houses and boats crowded into the harbour. The fine weather also means that people are in good spirits. From the promontory known as *The Island* you have a great view looking back at St Ives. In the mid-19th century, more and more artists were enticed into this naturally beautiful region, starting with William Turner. Many of them stayed and opened galleries. A train ride on the

Feel the wind in your hair: take a break at Porthmeor Beach Café in St Ives

Barbara Hepworth, Ben Nicholson or Paule Vézelay. It also showcases less well-known artists who are associated with St Ives. For those not so keen on modern art, there is a fabulous view over St Ives and the beach! *March–Oct daily 10am–5.20pm, Nov–Feb Tue–Sun 10am–4.20pm | admission £12, under 18s free | Porthmeor Beach | tate.org.uk/visit/tate-st-ives |* ⏱ *2–3 hrs*

PORTHMEOR STUDIOS

Much of what ends up hanging in the galleries of St Ives is created here. The workshops on the beach, which were formerly fishermen's cottages, have been occupied by artists for almost 150 years. The way the light falls and the view of the sea render these spaces a source of inspiration. You'll always stumble across an artist if you drop by – and there are also regular open days. *Back Road | bsjwtrust.co.uk*

BARBARA HEPWORTH MUSEUM

The former home of sculptor Barbara Hepworth is now a museum. You can learn more about her life and work here, and many of her sculptures are on show in the lovely gardens. *Tue–Sun 10am–4.20pm | admission £8 | combined ticket for £14.50 also includes admission to other local museums | Barnoon Hill | tate.org.uk |* ⏱ *1 hr*

St Ives Bay Line (daily | return from £4 | greatscenicrailways.co.uk) is probably the most pleasant approach route to the town, because it gives you the perfect view of the bay. The train connects St Erth and St Ives along the coast.

SIGHTSEEING

TATE ST IVES ⭐ ☂

The smaller sister of London's Tate, hidden away in remote Cornwall, is one of the most exciting art galleries in the country.

Right by Porthmeor Beach, the gallery displays changing exhibitions of contemporary art in a modern setting and also features works by the likes of

EATING & DRINKING

THE BEAN INN

This little vegetarian restaurant also serves plenty of vegan dishes, including pasta, vegetable cakes and soups.

It is attached to a guesthouse but is frequented by many non-guests too. *St Ives Road | tel. 01736 795918 | thebeaninn.co.uk | ££*

PORTHMEOR BEACH CAFÉ

You'll struggle to find a more pleasant spot for a bite to eat or a coffee: it's right on the beach, and almost every seat gives you a great view of the sea.

INSIDER TIP
Sand, sea and snacks

It also serves light bites – from tapas and fish to cream teas – as well as delicious drinks. The ingredients are, whenever possible, sourced from local producers. *Porthmeor Beach | tel. 01736 793366 | porthmeor-beach. co.uk | £££*

SHOPPING

Most shops can be found on *Fore Street*. It would be a crime to buy cheap mass-produced tat here. There are umpteen galleries selling not only paintings, but also things like postcards of art prints. The shop in Tate St Ives sells books, art prints, etc. and is well worth a look.

SPORT & ACTIVITIES

Watersports – particularly surfing – can be done on almost all beaches. On Porthmeor Beach, *St Ives Surf School (stivessurfschool.co.uk)* offers courses in surfing, kayaking and coasteering *(from £45)*. Roam *(roam cornwall.com)* does the same on the other side in Carbis Bay (almost 2km east).

BEACHES

You will find great beaches on both sides of the old town: *Porthgwidden Beach* and *Harbour Beach* – and *Porthmeor Beach*, as lovely as it is central. Here, people stretch out on the white sand and surf the waves in the clear waters, all against the backdrop of the lovely town. If you fancy something a little quieter, head to *Carbis Bay* – great for surfing.

NEWQUAY

(□ E8) **Don't expect too much of a surfers' paradise – except you will find high waves and a perfect beach.**

The typical small town of Newquay (pop. 20,000) is not Cornwall's most picturesque spot. But the long, sandy beaches are fantastic! It's best to take a whole afternoon to wander round – and make sure you swim in the sea. It gets busy in the summer, when hordes of backpackers descend on the place and transform Newquay into a British take on a surfers' paradise.

SIGHTSEEING

NEWQUAY ZOO

With numerous awards for sustainable tourism, Newquay Zoo is home to many rare animals. Over 130 species are found here, including lions, monkeys and penguins. *Daily April–Oct 10am–5pm, Nov–March 10am–4pm | admission £14.85 | Trenance Gardens | newquayzoo.org.uk | ⏱ 3 hrs*

EATING & DRINKING

THE BEACH HUT

This restaurant and bar in Watergate Bay Hotel has it all: delicious food – like burgers (including vegetarian) or crab linguine – with a great view of the sea and an upmarket but relaxed atmosphere. *On the beach | Watergate Bay | tel. 01637 860543 | watergate bay.co.uk/eat/the-beach-hut | ££*

THE GRIFFIN INN

This pub near the station may seem a bit rustic, but the kitchen serves delicious classics like fish and chips and burgers – washed down with a pint of local beer. *Cliff Road | tel. 01637 874067 | griffin-inn-newquay.co.uk | £*

SPORT & ACTIVITIES

The most popular beaches for surfing and other water sports are *Fistral Beach* and, slightly further away, *Watergate Bay*. You can hire surf boards and take surfing lessons with companies such as *Wave Hunters (Watergate Bay | tel. 07939 998213 | wavehunters.co.uk).*

FREEDIVE UK

The trendy new sport of mermaid diving will see you gliding through the water like Ariel, the little mermaid. Since this diving school started offering the course, the hype has been continuous (places sell out quickly!). *Full-day course £150/pers | tel. 01637 621922 | freediveuk.com*

INSIDER TIP
Under the sea

LEISURE WORLD

On rainy days, or if it's too cold in the sea, the kids can swim, slide and splash about in this leisure pool in Newquay. The water is heated to about 30°C ,and there is a 25m slide for adults. *Mon–Fri 6.30am–9pm, Sat 7am–5.30pm, Sun 8am–5pm | admission £6.50, children £4.50 | Trenance Leisure Park*

BEACHES

Newquay's picture-postcard beaches start in the town centre at *Great Western Beach*, a wonderful stretch of sand along the rocky shoreline. Slightly further away, *Watergate Bay* looks like something out of a film: big, beautiful, and with surfboard hire and upmarket dining.

WELLNESS

WATERGATE BAY HOTEL

This ultra-modern spa hotel is the perfect place to relax, right on the beach, with an infinity pool and all the trappings. The *day pass (£110)* includes a 60-minute treatment. *Tel. 01637 860543 | watergatebay.co.uk*

AROUND NEWQUAY

16 TRERICE

5km / 12 mins southeast of Newquay (by car)

Even Newquay gets rainy days sometimes. This fine Elizabethan manor house on the outskirts of Newquay is well worth a visit. You will notice the many Dutch elements, including the gables – a reminder of the time the designer spent in Holland. Inside, everything is furnished in Tudor style. The adjacent *Barn Restaurant (£)* in a converted barn is well known for its lemon cake. *March–Oct daily 11am–5pm | admission £11 | Kestle Mill | nationaltrust.org.uk/trerice |* ⏱ *1½ hrs |* 🛏 *E8*

🔟 LAPPA VALLEY STEAM RAILWAY 👫

7km / 15 mins south of Newquay (by car)

This 3km railway line near Newquay originally serviced a local mine. Now, it is a leisure park with steam engines. There is also a park nearby where you can go canoeing on the lake. *April–Oct daily 9.30am–5pm, Nov and Feb/March Sat/Sun 11.10am–4.15pm | tickets £15.95 (£8 in winter), families £55.50 | Benny Halt, St Newlyn East near Newquay | lappavalley.co.uk |* 🛏 *E9*

🔟 BEDRUTHAN STEPS

13km / 25 mins north of Newquay (by car)

Not far from Newquay, you will find Cornwall's most spectacular rocky coastline: single rock stacks rise from the sand near the rocky clifftops and form a pattern of steps. According to legend, the giant Bedruthan used to climb up them. The coast path leads right by here. *St Eval, Bedruthan | short. travel/cod15 |* 🛏 *E7*

Newquay is a top destination for surfers – refreshments with a view of the waves

EAST CORNWALL

CORNWALL'S RUGGED SIDE

With ruins and prehistoric legacies, you will discover a more mystical Cornwall in the east. The legend of King Arthur lingers over some of the sights – he was reputedly conceived in Tintagel. But even though it is only a legend, an entire region thrives on the story.

The picturesque village of Port Isaac is a little seaside gem

Small, enchanted villages are dotted amid the green and sometimes wild countryside. Time seems to have stood still in the little ports hidden along the coast. There is a good reason for this: many of the harbours were built to transport natural resources, but trading in these stopped many years ago.

The locals have made the best of this, and today they earn their living with authentic restaurants, quaint shops and cosy hotels – many with stunning sea views.

EAST CORNWALL

CELTIC SEA

13 Boscastle

Tintagel Castle ★ ● **Tintagel**
p. 74

Delabole

Camelford

12 **Port Isaac** ★ 🚲 ○ St Teath

Polzeath

Harbour Cove ☀

Rock Beach ☀ Pityme

11 Rock

● **Padstow**
p. 71

The Seafood
Restaurant ★

30km, 2 hrs

St Kew Highway

Bodieve

○ **Wadebridge**

Whitecross

39

39

30

Mount Charles ○

● **Bodmin**
p. 67

38

○ Trenance

○ Trevarrian

Tremayne

Lanivet ○

6 **Lanhydrock**

○ **St Columb Major**

CORNWALL

7 **Restormel Castle**

○ Lostwithiel

Quintrell Downs ○

30

○ Roche

Fraddon ○

St Dennis

391

Penhale

Nanpean

Stenalees ○

St Blazey

Golant ○

Foxhole

St Stephen

Polkerris Beach ☀

● **Fowey**
p. 69

St Austell ○

🚶 4½ km
1 hr

9 Polruan

Grampound Road ○

390

Gribbin Head ★ **10**

Grampound

London Apprentice

MARCO POLO HIGHLIGHTS

★ **CALSTOCK VIADUCT**
The spectacular railway bridge over the River Tamar. ➤ p. 65

★ **GRIBBIN HEAD**
Headland near Fowey with a fantastic coastal hiking path. ➤ p. 71

★ **THE SEAFOOD RESTAURANT**
TV chef Rick Stein showcases his talent here. ➤ p. 72

★ **PORT ISAAC**
Picturesque fishing village which often features in films. ➤ p. 73

★ **TINTAGEL CASTLE**
With or without King Arthur, this castle ruin on the coast is legendary. ➤ p. 74

LAUNCESTON

(□ J6) **A town with a proud aura – thanks to the castle ruins that loom above it: the centre of Launceston (pop. 11,700) has an important air about it, and for a good reason.**

Until the 19th century, the town was Cornwall's capital. Today, it's a pleasant little town with pretty shops and well-maintained buildings. The small streets around the High Street, Broad Street and Church Street are ideal for window shopping.

SIGHTSEEING

LAUNCESTON CASTLE

This ruined castle dates to the 11th century and was the centre of government in Cornwall for centuries. In the 16th century, it became a courthouse, and was the scene of the trial and execution of those involved in the Cornish rebellions. In 1973, it was here that King Charles III was proclaimed Duke of Cornwall. *April–Oct daily 10am–5pm | admission £6.80 | Castle Lodge | english-heritage.org.uk | ⏱ 1 hr*

LAWRENCE HOUSE 🐗

This museum is quirkier than you might expect: for example, chuck an old penny into the 19th-century jukebox… The 50 tunes you can choose from include "God Save the King"! And what does Lawrence/Cornwall have to do with Lawrence/Australia? At this museum, all will be revealed: the town in Tasmania was named after the first shipment of British prisoners to be sent down under. *April–Oct Mon–Fri 10.30am–4.30pm | free admission | 9 Castle Street | national trust.org.uk/lawrence-house | ⏱ 1 hr*

EATING & DRINKING

KING'S HEAD

This guesthouse serves all the British pub classics: from Sunday roast to fish and chips. And you can wash it all down with a pint of ale. *Five Lanes | tel. 01566 86241 | kingsheadlaunceston. co.uk | ££*

LIBERTY COFFEE

Tired of sightseeing? Take a well-earned break in this café. You can sample delicious cakes, light bites and perfectly prepared speciality coffee. *4 Northgate Street | tel. 01566 776751 | liberty-coffee.co.uk | £*

SPORT & ACTIVITIES

HIDDEN VALLEY – THE PUZZLE PARK 👥

This unusual park has lots to discover. Children can solve puzzles on the trail of Sherlock Holmes, find their way through a maze, discover secret doors and enjoy a ride on a miniature steam train. *April–Sept daily 10am–5pm | admission £18.50, children £17 (cheaper online) | Tredidon, St Thomas | hiddenvalley.co.uk*

AROUND LAUNCESTON

1 TREGUDDICK DISTILLERY

6km / 7 mins west of Launceston (by car)

One of England's youngest distilleries has opened on the site at Treguddick. Seventy different plant species are cultivated under plastic domes and are used primarily to flavour the gin. You can visit the premises – and try some gin – on one of their guided tours. *Daily 9.30am–5pm, tours 10.30am and 2.30pm | Treguddick | treguddick. com | ⬚ J6*

2 TAMAR VALLEY

35km / 30 mins south of Launceston (by car)

Much of the river valley extends along the border between Devon and Cornwall and is one of the most beautiful areas for hiking and cycling tours in this part of England. The Tamar Valley was once a mining region. But the mines have closed and the area has been discovered by weekend visitors. The ⭐ *Calstock Viaduct*, near the village of Calstock, is a great photo opportunity. At a height of 37m the viaduct serves as a railway bridge high above the river. For activities like zip-lining or archery, check out *Treesurfers (April–Oct | booking required | Tamar Trails Centre, Woodlands, Gulworthy | tel. 01822 833409 | treesurfers.co.uk). ⬚ K7*

An excursion to the Tamar Valley will take you to Calstock Viaduct

LISKEARD

(⬚ J8) **Liskeard (pop. 9,000) may not be Cornwall's most attractive town, but it is authentic.**

The *Guildhall Clock Tower* soars above the other typical Georgian and Victorian buildings. The picturesque *Liskeard and Looe Union Canal*, which was built in the 19th century for the mining industry, was closed in 1910. Now, hiking groups are attracted to the locks that have partly fallen into disrepair. Liskeard's wealth was generated from the region's copper mines. Nowadays, it has become a commercial centre – and one of the few places where a *Cattle Market (2 Fairpark Road)* is still held. It takes place every two weeks on Tuesdays.

Dreaming of adventures: Polperro used to be a smugglers' stomping ground

SIGHTSEEING

STUART HOUSE

Some people come here just for the little hidden garden, but if you go inside you can learn about local history. Charles I used the house in 1644 when he was preparing his troops for battle during the English Civil War. There is an exhibition about this period and a gallery showing art from the local area. *Mon–Sat 10am–3.30pm | free admission | Barras Street | stuart house.org.uk | ⏱ 1 hr*

EATING & DRINKING

HUB CAFÉ

Perfect for a tasty lunch: this café in a community centre serves exclusively vegetarian and vegan food – mainly home-made quiches, salads and pies. *Liskerrett Community Centre | Varley Lane | tel. 01579 340307 | liskerrett. co.uk/cafe | £*

LISKEARD TAVERN

A new gastropub, like so many that have sprung up all over the country, which is a little outside the town centre. Cosy up and enjoy the classics of British cuisine. *Haviland Road | tel. 01579 341752 | whitbreadinns.co.uk | ££*

SPORT & ACTIVITIES

ADRENALIN QUARRY 😛

Jump off a 50m clifftop and travel at 60kmh on a zip-line over a 500m-high ravine – this park is perfect for adrenalin junkies! Courage required, despite the safety harness. *April–Sept daily 10am–6pm, Oct–March Sat/Sun 10am–4pm | Lower Clicker Road, Menheniot near Liskeard | activities from £12 | adrenalinquarry.co.uk*

AROUND LISKEARD

3 TRETHEVY QUOIT
5km / 12 mins north of Liskeard (by car)

The 5,500-year-old dolmen, a table-top style tombstone, is also known as *Giant's House*. A 2.7m-high stone slab is held up by five other standing stones. It is on a much smaller scale than Stonehenge, but it's still impressive. *Always open | free admission | B3254 near Darite | english-heritage. org.uk | ⎙ J7*

4 LOOE
14km / 20 mins south of Liskeard (by car)

This pleasant coastal town with a harbour (pop. 5,300) on Cornwall's southern coast lies on both sides of the River Looe and offers a surprising array of shops. You can take the *Looe Valley Line (£5.80 per trip, £5.90 off-peak return | gwr.com)* and travel by train from Liskeard through the beautiful countryside to Looe. The guesthouse *Harbour Moon (Quayside)* offers lovely views of the river – as well as fresh beer and cider on tap. ⎙ J9

INSIDER TIP
Train journey with a view

5 POLPERRO
22km / 30 mins south of Liskeard (B3254)

If you would like to find out how Polperro (pop. 5,300) became a smuggler's paradise you should visit the local *Heritage Museum of Smuggling and Fishing (April–Oct daily 10.30am–4.30pm | admission £3 | Harbour Studio, The Warren)* in the harbour. The village still feels like a typical fishing port even though tourism, not fishing, is the main source of income these days. You can get a great overview of the place at 👥 *Polperro Model Village (April–Oct daily 10am–6pm | admission £3, children £1 | The Old Forge, Mill Hill | polperro modelvillage.com | ⏱ 2 hrs)*, which has recreated the village in miniature. Children will have a lot of fun learning about history here. ⎙ H9

BODMIN

(⎙ G8) **In Bodmin (pop. 15,000), you will experience real Cornish life.**

This small town on the fringes of Bodmin Moor, with its granite houses and shops along Fore Street, is something of a hub for the region. People come here to do their shopping, take care of official business, and also to celebrate the end of the work day in one of the pubs. After all, Bodmin was the capital of Cornwall for a short time in the 19th century – which partly explains the many elegant buildings that have been preserved to this day.

Beautiful Bodmin Moor: inspiration for writers and filmmakers

SIGHTSEEING

BODMIN JAIL

The former jail is now a fascinating tourist attraction, even if you're not enthusiastic about the history of executioners and prisoners. During World War II, the crown jewels were stored here for safekeeping. There are also ghost tours and other events. *Daily 9.30am–6.30pm | admission £18.50 | Berrycoombe Road | bodminjail.org |* ⏱ *1 hr*

BODMIN KEEP

This military museum is interesting for anyone who wants to immerse themselves in history. It explains all kinds of historical events and displays equipment from the region's army, especially uniforms, medals and weapons. *Tue–Sat 10am–5pm | admission £9 | Castle Canyke Road | bodminkeep.org.uk |* ⏱ *1 hr*

EATING & DRINKING

LANIVET INN

This rustic pub not only offers beers on tap but also a wide menu choice, from mussels and fish pie to vegetarian dishes. *Truro Road | tel. 01208 831212 | ££*

WOODS CAFÉ

Hidden away by a stream on the edge of woodland, this café's location couldn't be more idyllic. Here, you can drink tea grown in Cornwall – it comes from the Tregothnan Estate, a little further west, the first tea plantation in the UK. The café serves delicious home-made snacks and cakes, all freshly prepared. *Callywith Cottage, Cardinham Woods | tel. 01208 78111 | woodscafe.co.uk | ££*

INSIDER TIP
Local tea

AROUND BODMIN

6 LANHYDROCK

4km / 10 mins south of Bodmin (by car)

The magnificent Victorian country house is in the heart of an enchanted wooded estate and parkland. The library contains a book that is supposed to have helped Henry VIII with the annulment of his first marriage and thus was partly instrumental in the establishment of the Anglican Church. *House March–Oct daily 11am–5.30pm, Nov Sat/Sun and Dec daily 11am–4pm; park always open | admission £18 | nationaltrust.org.uk/ lanhydrock | ⏱ 2 hrs | ▥ G8*

7 RESTORMEL CASTLE

12km / 15 mins south of Bodmin (by car)

The circular shell keep of Restormel Castle, one of Cornwall's best-preserved Norman castles, is in a beautiful hilltop setting by the River Fowey. Although it is now a ruin, the outlook clearly indicates the once-strategic importance of this site; you can see far into the distance. *March–Oct daily 10am–4pm | admission £6.80 | Restormel Road | Lostwithiel | english-heritage.org.uk | ⏱ 1 hr | ▥ G8*

8 BODMIN MOOR

20km / 20 mins east of Bodmin (by car)

While everybody heads for Dartmoor, they overlook the smaller but equally impressive Bodmin Moor. It too boasts beautiful hiking trails and fabulous views, but perhaps not quite so many myths. Daphne du Maurier was inspired in the guesthouse *Jamaica Inn (Bolventor | tel. 01566 86250 | jamaicainn.co.uk | ££)* to write the novel of the same name that was later filmed by Alfred Hitchcock. There is also a small museum *(daily 8am–9pm | admission £3.95 | ⏱ 30 mins)* where you can learn more about the 300-year history of smugglers in this region with the help of pictures and other exhibits. In the southeastern region of the moor are the *Hurlers Stone Circles (always open | admission free | Minions, Liskeard | english-heritage.org.uk)*. According to legend, they were all men who were turned to stone as punishment for playing hurling on the Sabbath. ▥ H–J7

FOWEY

(▥ H9) **Every August, thousands of visitors are attracted to the Fowey Regatta in the small port, but Fowey (pop. 2,400) has plenty more to offer.**

The port was once one of the region's most important shipping centres for the transport of natural resources. Today, the town has many fine restaurants and expensive shops. The view of the houses nestled along the banks of the River Fowey down to the coast are beyond picturesque. The writer Daphne du Maurier lived for many years at the estate *Menabilly* (not open to the public) near Fowey and immortalised it in her novel *Rebecca,* later made into a film. In memory of the writer, the town has the small *Daphne du Maurier Literary Centre* and in May holds the annual *Fowey Festival (foweyfestival.com),* a week-long festival of arts and literature featuring world-famous writers and musicians.

SIGHTSEEING

ST CATHERINE'S CASTLE

The 15th-century St Catherine's Castle by the estuary has a magical aura about it. It is still relatively well preserved, largely thanks to its role in World War II, when its strategic position at the mouth of the River Fowey led to its use as an anti-aircraft post. The view of Fowey and the sea from here is wonderful. *Always open | free admission | St Catherine's Cove | english-heritage.org.uk |* ⏱ *1 hr*

EATING & DRINKING

THE GALLEON INN

Dinner by the water: make sure you get a seat outside and enjoy a pint by the Fowey River. You won't get fine dining here, but the place does serve hearty British pub food such as scampi, fish and lasagne. *12 Fore Street | tel. 01726 833014 | galleon-inn.co.uk | ££*

SAM'S

Fancy some seafood or sardines? Sam's has a relaxed, American feel to it but is one of the best fish restaurants in the area. Many people drop in just for a cocktail. *20 Fore Street | tel. 01726 832273 | samscornwall.co.uk | ££*

BEACHES

The most stunning beaches are on the other side of Gribbin Head peninsula, such as 🏖 *Polkerris Beach*, a little former port with a sandy beach, pub and restaurant. If you want something a bit nearer, *Readymoney Cove* on the southern edge of Fowey may be small, but it's very beautiful.

AROUND FOWEY

🟧 POLRUAN

0.5km / 5 mins east of Fowey (by ferry)

Polruan (pop. 600) is rather overshadowed by Fowey, but it is just as interesting. You can reach the small village on the east side of the River Fowey by taking the pleasant ferry crossing *(May–Sept Mon–Sat 7.15am–11pm, Sun 9am–11pm, Oct–April Mon–Sat 7.15am–7pm, Sun 10am–5pm | £2.80 | depending on scheduled times, from Whitehouse Pier or Town Quay | ctomsandson.co.uk/polruan-ferry). Blockhouse Fort (always open | free admission)* is almost a counterpart to St Catherine's Castle, though not as well preserved. The same applies to the ruins of the eighth-century *St Saviours Church* that sits majestically above the village.

🔟 GRIBBIN HEAD ⭐

7km / 12 mins southwest of Fowey (by car)

As you walk along this headland, southwest of Fowey, the fresh sea wind blows in your face. The 26m-high, red and white *Gribbin Tower* is a notable landmark, especially for mariners. From here you can enjoy panoramic sea views. 🗺 *G9*

PADSTOW

(🗺 F7) **If you could dream up an enchanted spot by a harbour, where you could spend the rest of your days, it would probably look like Padstow (pop. 3,000).**

The harbour is enclosed by small houses on three sides and the town centre, nestled behind the hill, has winding alleys and narrow streets. This town is for foodies: TV chef Rick Stein lives in Padstow for part of the year. He also owns about a dozen pubs, hotels and restaurants. This is Cornwall's centre for exceptional fish cuisine. If you fancy seeing Padstow a little livelier than usual, come on 1 May. Every year on this day, the town celebrates the *Obby Oss Festival* with plenty of dancing, music and, of course, food.

INSIDER TIP
Horsing around in May!

Stripy landmark: the Gribbin Tower

rather quiet and peaceful life. Fishermen still put out to sea from here. The *Padstow–Rock Ferry (daily 8am–5pm, in summer until 8pm | £3 per trip | padstow-harbour.co.uk)* operates all year between the harbour and the opposite bank of the River Camel. It's worth taking the trip if only for the views of Padstow from the water.

PRIDEAUX PLACE

Every corner of this house is magnificent: Prideaux Place is a manor with elegant interiors and traditional wood panelling. The owners still live here, so opening times are limited. The wonderful parkland is home to one of England's oldest herds of deer. *April–Sept Mon–Fri 10.30am–4.30pm | admission £5 | Tregirls Lane | prideaux place.co.uk |* ⏱ *2 hrs*

SIGHTSEEING

QUAYSIDE

The harbour has always been the heart of Padstow. It's the hub for the town's

EATING & DRINKING

THE SEAFOOD RESTAURANT ★

Probably the best restaurant in England as far as fish and seafood are concerned. Many of the dishes served at Rick Stein's restaurant were swimming in the sea just a short while before. Stein collected his recipes from all over the world during his travels for the BBC. *Riverside | tel. 01841 532700 | rickstein.com | £££*

STEIN'S FISH & CHIPS

The cheaper version of Stein's fine cuisine: in this restaurant, you can enjoy…fish & chips! *South Quay | tel. 01841 532700 | rickstein.com | ££*

SHOPPING

It's incredible how many fashion boutiques there are in this small town! They are mainly on the west side of the harbour in *Church Lane* and *Cross Street*.

SPORT & ACTIVITIES

Padstow Cycle hire (4–6 South Quay | padstowcyclehire.com) rents out bicycles, which you can use to take a lovely ride along the coast.

BEACHES

St George's Cove, right by Padstow, is beautiful and expansive. The pleasant sandy beach 🐾 *Harbour Cove* will provide some peace and quiet.

AROUND PADSTOW

🅚 ROCK

2km / 10 mins east of Padstow (by ferry)

This small village (pop. 1,200) lies on the other side of the River Camel from Padstow. Its nickname is "Chelsea-on-Sea", after London's elegant district, and it is a popular though rather exclusive destination for day trips. This is evident from the fine cuisine.

INSIDER TIP
Classy day trip

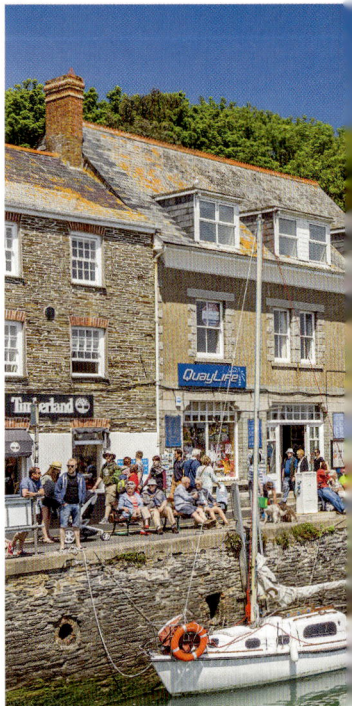

However, Rock's original attraction was its long ✈ beach – great for walks at low tide – and numerous water sports activities: sailing, surfing, water-skiing and canoeing – everything is possible. Nearby is *Polzeath*, whose flat beach attracts visitors from across the county – especially surfers. The surf is usually excellent here. *F7*

🅱 PORT ISAAC ★

A charming and picturesque fishing village – this is probably why Port Isaac (pop. 700) repeatedly features as a backdrop for films and television series – perhaps most famously the 10 seasons (over a period of 18 years) of *Doc Martin*. Down the centuries, the village was a relatively important harbour for the local quarries. Nowadays, it has become a tourist centre – especially since the local sea shanty choir *Fisherman's Friends* got a record deal with an international label and the whole thing was turned into a film by Chris Foggin in 2019. Its narrow lanes, which wind their way to the waterside, are perfect for atmospheric photos. ⚑ You can enjoy a cream tea in an original setting, a former chapel from the 19th century, *Chapel Café (Port Isaac Pottery, Roscarrock Hill | tel. 01208 881300 | £)*. *G7*

Padstow harbour: Great atmosphere and delicious fish dishes

Tintagel Castle: ruined walls, lots of steps and spectacular views

TINTAGEL

(□ G6) **A small village (pop. 700) which mainly thrives because of an age-old legend: King Arthur was supposedly conceived here at Tintagel Castle.**

The monarch is said to have gained victory for the Britons in so many battles. However, historians believe that the evidence is lacking and the king may never have existed. But that makes no difference in Tintagel. The town is doing just fine, if the busloads of visitors are anything to go by. They arrive here all year to embark on the trail of the fabled king. Their visits are handsomely rewarded in this location:

the impressive countryside offers one of the most ruggedly beautiful sections of coastline in southern England.

SIGHTSEEING

TINTAGEL CASTLE ★

This castle is the best evidence for Arthur never having been born – at least not here: it dates to the 13th century and the legends of King Arthur date from the fifth century. Today, there are only a few walls remaining of Tintagel Castle, but its setting is unique. You cross a narrow bridge to reach a rocky headland and the ruins of the iconic castle. The view more than compensates for the numerous steps you have to climb. *April–Sept daily 10am–6pm, March and Oct Wed–Sun 10am–4pm, Nov–Feb Sat/Sun 10am–4pm | admission £14.80 | Castle Road | english-heritage.org.uk | ⏱ 2 hrs*

OLD POST OFFICE

For a long time, this 14th-century farmhouse was home to Tintagel post office, hence the name. The National Trust has now restored the premises to its former state as a traditional house, where you can see what life was like in the Middle Ages and even look at some Victorian post paraphernalia. *Daily March–Sept 10.30am–5.30pm, Feb and Oct 11am–4pm | admission £6.50 | Fore Street | nationaltrust.org.uk | ⏱ 30 mins*

EATING & DRINKING

CHARLIE'S CAFÉ & RESTAURANT

The breakfasts are scrumptious, the scones are heavenly, the fish burger a dream, the salads divine – this restaurant in Tintagel centre will fortify you for your climb to the castle. *Fore Street | tel. 01840 779500 | charlies.cafe | ££*

THE CORNISH BAKERY

A wonderful small café on the way to the castle. Cornish pasties, Danish pastries and excellent coffee – get something to take away and enjoy it on the coast. *1a Castle Road | £*

SHOPPING

You can hardly avoid trying the local **INSIDER TIP** **A creamy tipple** clotted cream while you're here, but have you ever tried Clotted Cream Gin? It is produced at the *Wrecking Coast Distillery (The Old Bookshop, Atlantic Road | thewreckingcoastdistillery.com)*: the gin has a gentle flavour with a hint of juniper and is available in several shops in Tintagel.

AROUND TINTAGEL

🔞 BOSCASTLE

6km / 10 mins northeast of Tintagel (by car)

Boscastle (pop. 800) has a perfect setting in a romantic valley at the confluence of the River Valency and the River Jordan. But in 2004, it was this very location that led to disastrous flooding in the area. Things have now returned to normal. Old houses flank both riverbanks and the harbour nestles into the hillsides almost like an open-air theatre. Legends once circulated here about witches and myths, and these are presented in the small *Museum of Witchcraft and Magic (April–Oct daily 10am–5.30pm | admission £7 | museumofwitchcraftandmagic.co.uk | ⏱ 1 hr).* 🗺 *G6*

🔞 BUDE

30km / 30 mins north of Tintagel (by car)

The small village (pop. 7,700) in the extreme north of Cornwall is popular because of its beaches with the traditional brightly coloured beach huts. In *Bude Castle (April–Oct daily 10am–5pm, Nov–March 10am–4pm | free admission | The Castle | thecastlebude.org.uk | ⏱ 2 hrs)* there is an interesting exhibition about the history of this region, its geology and the shipwrecks off the coast. There is also an art gallery. Don't hang around there too long, though, because you need to visit *Life is a Beach (Summerleaze Beach | ££).* **INSIDER TIP** **Sundowner anyone?** The hip beach café with a view of the sea almost makes you feel like you're in Hawaii – light bites, delicious beer and picture-perfect sunsets.

SOUTH DEVON

BETWEEN THE MOOR AND THE SEA

South Devon doesn't go in for half measures: it has the most famous hiking area in the southwest, Dartmoor; and its "English Riviera" near Torquay might well be the best-known bathing area in England. What's more, it is home to Exeter and Plymouth, the biggest and liveliest cities in Devon.

Plymouth isn't just the largest city in the county, it's also the maritime hub of the entire country in historical terms. Great seafarers like Sir Francis Drake set off from here on their voyages across the ocean,

There's plenty of room for hiking and chasing legends on Dartmoor

and emigrants came to the port on their way to starting a new life in America. It is still one of the most important bases for the British Navy today.

The myths of Dartmoor have inspired sagas and stories of mystery and intrigue. But, ultimately, the moor is simply a beautiful place for hiking, with its quaint villages and relics from a bygone age. While South Devon's multiple beaches – Torquay alone has several – feature palm trees and warmer weather.

SOUTH DEVON

Witheridge

Lapford

Morchard Bishop

Cadbury

Monkokehampton

Hatherleigh

North Tawton

Bow

Copplestone

Thorverton

377

Crediton

Jacobstowe

Folly Gate

Newton St Cyres

Cowley

16 Okehampton

30

Cheriton Bishop

Exeter Cathedral ★

Meldon

Whiddon Down

Crockernwell

Exeter
p. 80

Sourton

Lydford

DEVON

Chagford

Moretonhampstead

Go Ape 2

386

Manaton

Chudleigh

Mary Tavy

Postbridge

Widecombe
in the Moor

Bovey Tracey

Dartmoor ★

Ideford Combe

p. 94

Dartmeet

Newton Abbot

35km, 35 mins

Tavistock

Princetown

38

Horrabridge

Ashburton

380

Yelverton

Buckfastleigh

Kingskerswell

13 Buckland Abbey

Torquay
p. 85

Roborough

Totnes

72km, 50 mins

Marldon

Barbican ★

South Brent

Paignton 6

12km,
25 mins

Broadsands Beach

Plympton

52km, 55 mins

Brixham 7

14 Saltram

38

Ivybridge

Greenway ★ 9

Plymouth
p. 91

Lee Mill

Yealmpton

Ermington

Woodlands 10

Dartmouth
p. 88

8 Kings-
wear

Modbury

Newton Ferrers

Dartmouth Steam Railway ★

Churchstow

Burgh Island ★ 15

Bigbury Bay

Kingsbridge

Chillington

Torcross

Malborough

12 Salcombe

11 Start Point
Lighthouse

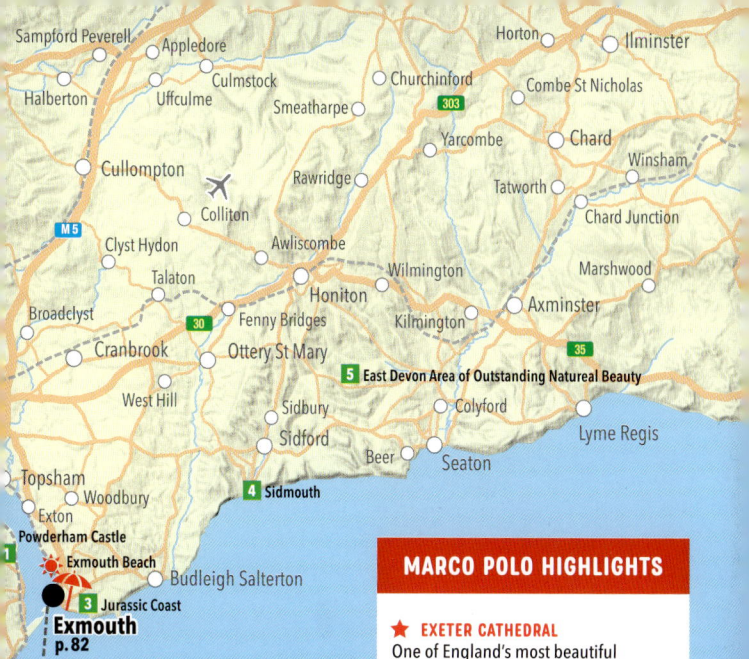

MARCO POLO HIGHLIGHTS

★ **EXETER CATHEDRAL**
One of England's most beautiful cathedrals, in the heart of Exeter.
➤ p. 80

★ **DARTMOUTH STEAM RAILWAY**
Old steam engines cruise between Paignton and Kingswear. ➤ p. 88

★ **GREENWAY**
For many years, Agatha Christie spent her summers at this beautiful house on the River Dart. ➤ p. 89

★ **BARBICAN**
Time seems to have stood still in the old harbour district of Plymouth – well, almost. ➤ p. 91

★ **BURGH ISLAND**
The small tidal island is home to the legendary Burgh Island Hotel – Agatha Christie described it in one of her books. ➤ p. 94

★ **DARTMOOR**
Isolation, heather moors and a perfect crime-thriller atmosphere amid the mystical landscape of this national park. ➤ p. 94

EXETER

(□ O5) **Exeter (pop. 125,000), Devon's capital, was heavily bombed in the Blitz during World War II, but the character of the important trading centre was mostly preserved.**

In the main shopping area along the High Street, you will notice buildings in various architectural styles that are from Tudor times, and parts of the city wall date back to the Romans. If you think that makes the city sound old and stuffy, you'd be wrong! Exeter is younger than you expect: over 20,000 students attend the University of Exeter, and it has a vibrant nightlife. ◆ There are free guided tours of the city every day at 11am and 2pm with *Red Coat Guided Tours (Hooker statue in front of the cathedral | tel. 01392 265203 | exeter.gov.uk).*

SIGHTSEEING

EXETER CATHEDRAL ⭐

You have to marvel at Exeter's Cathedral Church of Saint Peter (built 1275–1369), which sits on the green at Cathedral Yard and is obviously the most impressive building in the city centre. The west front of the sandstone building presents a wealth of biblical statues and above it is a wonderful traceried window. Inside you should look at the Gothic fan-vaulted ceiling, which is among the longest of its kind. There are free guided tours of the building several times a day. *Mon–Sat 9am–5pm, Sun 11.30am–4pm | admission £7.50 | 1 The Cloisters | exeter-cathedral.org.uk |* ⏱ *1 hr | □ d2–3*

ROYAL ALBERT MEMORIAL MUSEUM

The extensively renovated neo-Gothic building is much more than a local museum. You can visit the major exhibition on the history of Great Britain and specifically the region around Exeter. The art collection also has an excellent reputation countrywide. The museum bears the name of Queen Victoria's husband, Prince Albert. *Tue–Sun 10am–5pm | free admission | Queen Street | rammuseum.org.uk |* ⏱ *1–2 hrs | □ c2*

UNDERGROUND PASSAGES

These subterranean passages reveal history: visitors can walk beneath the High Street through the old 14th-century tunnels designed to carry water and enjoy a different view of Exeter. The passages are narrow, damp and dark, but you can also see the ruins of the old city gate. *Thu–Sun 10am–4pm | admission £7.50 | 2 Paris Street (entrance by Next) |* ⏱ *1 hr | □ d2*

> ### WHERE TO START?
>
> **Exeter Cathedral** *(□ d2–3):* if you are coming by car, it's best to leave it in the car park at John Lewis and stroll down the High Street to Queen Street. Turn left and the alley will lead you directly to the cathedral.

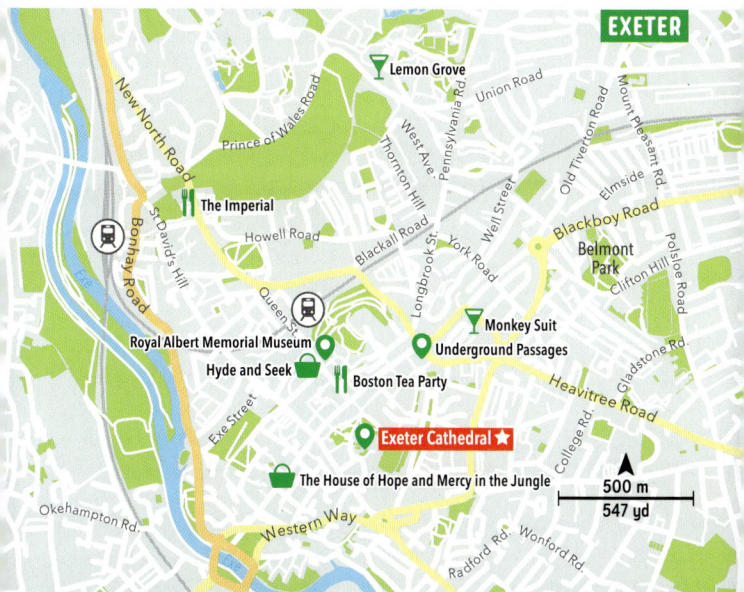

EXETER

Lemon Grove

New North Road

Prince of Wales Road

West Ave

Pennsylvania Rd.

Union Road

Old Tiverton Road

Mount Pleasant Rd.

The Imperial

St David's Hill

Bonhay Road

Howell Road

Thornton Hill

Blackall Road

Longbrook St.

York Road

Well Street

Elmside

Blackboy Road

Belmont Park

Clifton Hill Rd.

Polsloe Road

Queen St.

Royal Albert Memorial Museum

Monkey Suit

Underground Passages

Hyde and Seek

Boston Tea Party

Gladstone Rd.

Heavitree Road

Exe Street

Exeter Cathedral ★

College Rd.

The House of Hope and Mercy in the Jungle

500 m
547 yd

Okehampton Rd.

Western Way

Radford Rd.

Wonford Rd.

EATING & DRINKING

BOSTON TEA PARTY

Whether you're looking for breakfast, lunch or afternoon tea, this coffee shop in the town centre, popular with students, serves good coffee, fresh juices and a wide range of tasty, mostly organic dishes. *84 Queen Street | tel. 01392 201181 | boston teaparty.co.uk | £ | ☐ c2*

THE IMPERIAL

Large but inviting pub in a former hotel high above St David's railway station. 🐷 The food is cheap, though it won't be winning any awards, and it has one major advantage: you can order food until late in the evenings. In summer visitors can enjoy a pint in the pleasant beer garden outside.

New North Road | tel. 01392 434050 | £ | ☐ b1

SHOPPING

Exeter's town centre, along the High Street, offers all kinds of shops from the *John Lewis Department Store (1 Sidwell Street | ☐ d2)* to smaller shops at the opposite end of the pedestrian area.

THE HOUSE OF HOPE AND MERCY IN THE JUNGLE

Some people believe this is the best tea shop in Devon. Either way, you can treat yourself to delicious varieties from Oolong to Earl Grey, as well as excellent customer service. *1–3 McCoys Arcade, Fore Street | thehouseofhope andmercyinthejungle.co.uk | ☐ c3*

HYDE AND SEEK

You are guaranteed to come away from this gift shop with a souvenir of some sort, perhaps in the form of an art print featuring Exeter or Devon, a clock, a candle holder or a mug. *Unit 1, Harlequins, 1 Paul Street | hydeseek. co.uk | □ c2*

NIGHTLIFE

LEMON GROVE

This little concert and party venue is located on the main university campus. If you're after big names in music, look no further. *St German's Road | □ 0*

MONKEY SUIT

You can chill out with a cocktail or enjoy a craft beer at this bar that resembles someone's living room, complete with leather sofas and lamps. *161 Sidwell Street | themonkey suit.co.uk | □ e1*

AROUND EXETER

■ POWDERHAM CASTLE

13km / 20 mins south of Exeter (via the A379)

The home of the Earl of Devon has the appearance of a medieval castle. Built between 1390 and 1420, much of the castle is preserved. Inside there are secret doors and numerous items of original furniture. The castle grounds feature substantial gardens, including a knot garden. Don't miss the estate's *Farm Store (powderhamfarmshop.co.uk)* where you can find locally grown produce and a large selection of gardening-related souvenirs. *April–Oct Sun–Fri 11am–4pm | admission £14.95 | Kenton | powderham.co.uk | ⏱ 2 hrs | □ O6*

INSIDER TIP
Take home a piece of Devon

■ GO APE 🐒

14km / 15 mins south of Exeter (via the A38)

Swing like a monkey: at this park near Exeter, you can go zip trekking and hang out in the trees until you're breathless. The only condition: visitors must be at least ten years old and 1.40m tall. *April–Oct daily 9am–5pm, Feb/March and Nov Sat/Sun 9am–4pm (in good weather – it is recommended to check the website beforehand!) | admission adults from £33, children £18 | Haldon Forest Park, Bullers Hill, Kennford | goape.co.uk | □ O6*

EXMOUTH

(□ P6) The elegant Victorian houses along the promenade at Exmouth (pop. 33,000), with its 3km stretch of sandy beach, reflect the heyday of the town following the arrival of the railway link.

The previously faded old port has been renovated with a mix of brightly coloured houses, and the small boats in the marina offer a romantic setting on warm summer evenings. Many visitors come here primarily because the

Noble, ancient and featuring its own park: Powderham Castle

Jurassic Coast begins at nearby rocky Orcombe Point (see p. 84).

SIGHTSEEING

A LA RONDE

Who would have imagined building a 16-sided house? The two cousins Jane and Mary Parminter loved eccentric things, as you will notice from this curiously shaped 18th-century building. They not only designed their house but also some striking furniture inside. No fewer than 20 rooms are arranged around an octagonal centre. The house is still furnished exactly how it was left by the two women. *Feb–Oct daily 11am–5pm | admission £10.50 | Summer Lane | nationaltrust. org. uk/a-la-ronde | ⏱ 1 hr*

EATING & DRINKING

BUMBLE AND BEE

The menu may not be fit for a romantic dinner, but this stylish little café is perfect for breakfast, lunch or afternoon tea. You can get fluffy pancakes, delicious baked potatoes and fresh scones. The chef only uses seasonal and locally sourced products. *Manor Gardens | Alexandra Terrace | tel. 07791 229741 | bumbleandbee.co.uk | ££*

RIVER EXE CAFÉ

Probably the town's most unusual restaurant is on a barge that floats offshore in the Exe Estuary. Dishes include fresh seafood and vegetarian options, all prepared with locally sourced produce. *The Docks | accessed by water taxi (April–Oct, £5 return)*

AROUND EXMOUTH

Boats and unusual rock formations on the Jurassic Coast by Sidmouth

from Point Bar Grill on the marina | tel. 07761 116103 | riverexecafe.com | £££

SPORT & ACTIVITIES

Exmouth is a ⚑ centre for water sports enthusiasts and a wide range of activities is available, from surfing to canoeing and rowing. You can hire equipment at several points along the promenade such as *Exmouth Watersports (The Esplanade | tel. 01395 276599 | exmouthwatersports. co.uk).*

BEACHES

🐾 Exmouth Beach is beautiful, with 3km of golden sand for your enjoyment.

3 JURASSIC COAST

3 km / 7 mins east of Exmouth (via Marine Drive)

Scientists can read the cliffs along the *Jurassic Coast* like a book of geology. For everyone else this 150km stretch of coastline offers primarily one thing: stunning scenery with sensational rocky cliffs. From Orcombe Point near Exmouth to Old Harry Rocks in Dorset you will discover many different aspects of this UNESCO World Heritage Site, including the unusual red sandstone clifftops in East Devon. Near Beer, you can explore the limestone caves. The Jurassic Coast acquired its name from the many fossils found here dating from the Jurassic period. Guided fossil tours can be booked in neighbouring Dorset at the *Charmouth Heritage Coast Centre (specified dates, booking required) | £8 | Lower Sea Lane, Charmouth | tel. 01297 560772 | charmouth.org).* 📖 *P–S 5–6*

4 SIDMOUTH

18km / 30 mins northeast of Exmouth (by car)

One of the jewels on the *Jurassic Coast* is Sidmouth (pop. 13,000), nestled along the red sandstone cliffs and protected by grassy headlands. From the main beach, you can climb the wooden steps of *Jacob's Ladder* to *Connaught Gardens*, a pleasant garden on the sandstone clifftop. The

Clock Tower Café (Peak Hill Road | tel. 01395 515319 | clocktowercafes idmouth.co.uk | £) at the top of the hill not only offers panoramic sea views but provides a mouth-watering selection of home-made cakes and small plates. Q6

5 EAST DEVON AREA OF OUTSTANDING NATURAL BEAUTY

20km / 30 mins northeast of Exmouth (via the B3178)

The 260km² area near Seaton is known for its undulating grasslands and small woodlands. It is classified as one of Great Britain's *Areas of Outstanding Natural Beauty* and enjoys special protection. The area from Exmouth and Lyme Regis stretches inland from the *Jurassic Coast*. It is ideal for hiking and the region can also be explored on an old railway line: *Seaton Tramway (April–Oct daily 10am–4pm, scheduled dates in winter | £11.80 | Riverside Depot | Harbour Road | Seaton | tel. 01297 20375 | tram.co.uk)* runs about 5km from the coast to Colyton. Q–R 5–6

TORQUAY

(*O7–8*) **Torquay (pop. 65,000), once a magnificent seaside resort, may look a little run down but tourists still arrive by the busload.**

It is often regarded as a town for retirees and yet it is a popular tourist destination thanks to the picturesque bay and geological conditions – the locals say that Torquay, like Rome, is built on seven hills. In fact, there are almost 40 hills. The beaches are fabulous and the pedestrian zone is also a busy hub in south Devon. The "Queen of Crime", Agatha Christie, was born here in 1890. Every September a literature festival is held here in her honour.

SIGHTSEEING

TORRE ABBEY

This wonderful mixture of medieval abbey and Georgian country manor is home to a fascinating museum which tells the history of the region. Torre Abbey was founded as a monastery in 1196 and during the 15th century developed into one of the wealthiest of its kind in all England – until Henry VIII ordered the Dissolution of the Monasteries of England and Wales in the 16th century. The garden is especially interesting as it contains plants that were used as poisons in the novels of Agatha Christie. *April–Oct Tue–Sun 10am–5pm | admission £9.50 | The Kings Drive | torre-abbey. org.uk | 2 hrs*

KENTS CAVERN

The caves are a fantastic contrast to Torquay's summer beach life. Scientists have discovered objects dating back more than 450,000 years and they provide evidence of some of the earliest human activity in Britain. An upper jawbone discovered in Kents

Fine glassmaking at the artisan market in Cockington Court, Torquay

Cavern is believed to be more than 40,000 years old, making it (according to some scientists) the oldest evidence of modern man in Europe. In August, the cave is transformed into a cinema for a couple of days, showing mainly Hollywood classics from *Star Wars* to *Indiana Jones*. Daily 10am–5pm | admission £16 | 91 Ilsham Road | kents-cavern. co.uk | 🕐 1–2 hrs

INSIDER TIP
Star Wars in a cave

EATING & DRINKING

THE IMPERIAL HOTEL

This elegant 19th-century hotel has welcomed umpteen famous faces – probably partly because it offers the best afternoon tea in town. A fabulous place to enjoy tea, scones and all the trimmings, with views overlooking the harbour. *Park Hill Road* | tel. 01803 294301 | the imperialtorquay.co.uk | £££

INSIDER TIP
Time for tea!

NO. 7

This excellent little fish restaurant on the harbourside is a cosy affair. The products are locally sourced from the region and guests choose the fresh fish before it is prepared. *7 Beacon Hill* | tel. 01803 295055 | no7-fish.com | £££

SHOPPING

Fleet Street, with its shopping centre *Fleet Walk,* is the town's main shopping area. Many chains have opened branches of their stores here. *Cockington Court (cockingtoncourt. org)* slightly outside town has a pleasant craft centre, where you can buy souvenirs like wrought-iron hooks, wooden toys and glassware.

SPORT & ACTIVITIES

You can swim almost everywhere here, but *Shoalstone Pool*, set into the cliffs of Brixham, is a particularly beautiful spot. You can play tennis at *St Mary's Park* (Brixham), *Cary Park Tennis Club* (Babbacombe) and *Torre Abbey Leisure Park* in Torquay. *Torbay Sea School* in Brixham offers sailing courses.

SPLASHDOWN QUAYWEST 👯

The biggest outdoor waterpark in Britain offers plenty of attractions with eight waterslides and spectacular views. *May–Sept daily 9am–5pm | admission from £15.50, depending on time of year | Tanners Road, Goodrington Sands, Paignton | splashdownwaterparks.co.uk/quaywest | 🏠 O8*

BEACHES

There are about a dozen beaches along the bay of Torbay, some of them are sandy and others shingle. The best are the narrow 🐾 *Broadsands* with its little multicoloured beach huts (very photogenic!) and *Paignton Beach*. Not far from Torquay railway station, *Corbyn Bay*, with its wooden huts, is wonderfully quirky.

AROUND TORQUAY

6 PAIGNTON

6km / 10 mins south of Torquay (by car)

Torquay's little sister has the unfortunate reputation of being a cheap seaside resort. But Paignton (pop. 50,000) has several worthwhile attractions such as *Oldway Mansion (daily 9.30am–4.30pm | free admission | Torquay Road)*. This country estate was built at the end of the 19th century by the American Isaac Merritt Singer, of sewing machine fame. On the upper floor, there is a hall of mirrors in the style of the Palace of Versailles and outside there's a vast park. *Dartmouth Steam Railway* (see p. 88) leaves Paignton's *Queens Park Station* for Dartmouth (10.8km). 🏠 *O8*

7 BRIXHAM

13km / 20 mins south of Torquay (by car)

The picturesque town of Brixham (pop. 16,000), to the south of Torbay, has survived on its fishing industry for almost 1,000 years. Its colourful houses and small boats make for a striking scene along the water. The *Fish Market (tours on fixed dates, usually Wed mornings | therockfish. co.uk/products/fish-market-tour)* is near what is still an important port for local fishing boats. By the harbour, there are excellent restaurants like the

INSIDER TIP
Catch of the day

modern *Rockfish (The Harbour | tel. 01803 850872 | therockfish.co.uk | ££)* with great views over the bay. There is also a replica of Francis Drake's flagship, the *Golden Hind (March–Oct daily 10am–4pm | admission £6 | The Quay | goldenhinde.co.uk). 🕮 O8*

DARTMOUTH

(🕮 O9) **The best view of Dartmouth (pop. 5,000) is from the water – so make sure you take a trip in one of the small ferries at some point.**

Rows of pastel-coloured houses climb the green hills, while boats bob up and down in the harbour all year round. For centuries, Dartmouth was one of the country's major deep-water ports and it has been a Royal Navy base since the 14th century. Officers are still trained here today, and the magnificent *Britannia Royal Naval College* sits majestically above the town.

SIGHTSEEING

DARTMOUTH CASTLE
The imposing fortress – one of the most attractive of its kind – sits on the promontory on the Dart Estuary. At the highest point, there is a breathtaking view across the river. Dartmouth Castle once protected the vital waterway leading inland. *April–Oct daily 10am–5pm, Nov–March Sat/Sun 10am–4pm | admission £8.10 | Castle Road | english-heritage.org.uk | ⏱ 1 hr*

EATING & DRINKING

THE ANGEL
Fancy some lamb, halibut or apple soufflé? This restaurant in an old building on the river is one of the finest in Dartmouth serving much-lauded cuisine. *2 South Embankment | tel. 01803 833488 | theangel dartmouth.co.uk | £££*

BAYARDS COVE INN
At this old half-timbered house in the city centre, you can experience the classics of British cuisine with a slightly modern twist, and at reasonable prices. Fish, steak and tofu burgers are served with Instagram-worthy presentation. *27 Lower Street | tel. 01803 839278 | bayardscoveinn.co.uk | ££*

AROUND DARTMOUTH

🎱 KINGSWEAR
0.5km / 5 mins east of Dartmouth (by ferry)
The small village (pop. 1,200) on the river opposite Dartmouth has quaint and colourful cottages. This picturesque setting is a lovely place for a walk. The steam engines of the ⭐ *Dartmouth Steam Railway (several times a week | return £21 | Kingswear Station, The Square | tel. 01803 555872 | dartmouthrailriver.co.uk)* travels from here to Paignton. *Ferries (Mon–Sat 7.30am–11pm, Sun 9am–*

Full steam ahead from Kingswear to Paignton on the Dartmouth Steam Railway

11pm | £1.50 per trip | dartmouthrail river.co.uk) connect Kingswear with Dartmouth about every 15 minutes during the day. 🚍 O9

9 GREENWAY ⭐

10km / 25 mins north of Dartmouth (by ferry)

The picturesque house on the River Dart belonged to Agatha Christie for many years. She spent the summers here, where she perfected some of her best-selling stories, although she didn't write any here. However, Greenway features in her book *Dead Man's Folly*. The bright country house is still filled with all kinds of items that were kept here during Christie's time – including personal photos and her Order of the British Empire. You can stroll through the wonderful garden past a Victorian greenhouse and the boathouse by the river. The National Trust also rents holiday cottages on the estate, so you can get closer than ever to the "Queen of Crime". *March–Oct daily 10.30am–5pm, Nov/Dec Sat/Sun (daily between Christmas and New Year) 11am–4pm | admission £14 | Greenway Road, Galmpton | parking must be pre-booked by telephone; easy to reach by boat (March–Oct, £12 return) | tel. 0844 335 1287 (*) | nationaltrust.org.uk/greenway |* ⏱ *hrs* | 🚍 *O8*

INSIDER TIP
Being Miss Marple

10 WOODLANDS

10km / 12 mins west of Dartmouth (via the A3122)

Devon's largest theme park is ideal for families, with its giant swingboats and slides. The park has special animal

A small town nestled in rolling landscape: Salcombe lies on the Kingsbridge Estuary

zones and dinosaur trails. *April–Oct daily, Nov–March Sat/Sun 9.30am–5pm | admission £21.90, children under 110cm tall £16.90 (off season £12.45 each)|Woodlands Leisure Park, Blackawton, Totnes | woodlandspark. com | ⊞ N9*

🆔 START POINT LIGHTHOUSE
30km / 40 mins south of Dartmouth (via the A379)
The area around Freshwater Bay is one of the most beautiful spots in Devon for coastal walks, with green meadows on one side and jutting cliffs on the other. A path leads to Start Point Lighthouse, a white tower that was built on a spectacular clifftop and has been guiding ships through the English Channel since 1836. It has been automated since 1993 and can

be visited on certain days *April–Oct | Admission £8.50 | startpointdevon. co.uk | ⊞ N10*

🆔 SALCOMBE
30km / 45 mins southwest of Dartmouth (via the A381)
Romantic Salcombe (pop. 2,000) on Kingsbridge Estuary offers plenty of photo opportunities. The small, old houses are concentrated in the centre of town and there are two beaches by the river: *North Sands* and *South Sands*. In the pink-striped shop *Cranch (78 Fore Street)* you can enjoy a moment of nostalgia – since 1869, the store has sold brightly coloured sweets here. At the *Salcombe Gin School,* you can learn the basics of making your own gin,

INSIDER TIP
DIY gin

and the distillery on site *(Mon–Thu 10am–5pm, Fri/Sat 10am–10pm, Sun 11am–5pm | courses must be booked in advance | The Boathouse, 28 Island Street | tel. 01548 288180 | salcombe gin.com)* has plenty to see – and drink! *N10*

PLYMOUTH

(L9) **The old maritime town of Plymouth (pop. 260,000) in the far west of Devon has immense charm and its ports still radiate an atmosphere of openness towards the outside world.**

The rest of the town grew up in the 1950s – after heavy bombing during the World War II Blitz. As a result, the town's architecture is more functional than attractive. Sir Francis Drake, James Cook and Charles Darwin all put to sea from Plymouth and it's here the Royal Navy still maintains the largest military port in Western Europe. And if you fancy a shopping trip, look no further than the city's pedestrian zone in the centre!

WHERE TO START?

Barbican district *(d–e 5–6)*: it's best to park at one of the car parks on Lambhay Hill, then you can relax and explore the old harbour with its narrow streets. From here you can stroll to the limestone cliff at the Hoe and enjoy a fantastic panoramic view of the harbour.

SIGHTSEEING

BARBICAN ⭐

The old harbour is Plymouth's jewel. A walk along the quayside, where not much seems to have changed down the centuries, is like stepping back in time; only the boats in the harbour look modern. Stop off at one of the pubs or restaurants in the area. *Black Friars Distillery (Mon 10am–4.30pm, Tue–Sat 11am–5.30pm, Sun noon–5pm | tours from £15 | 60 Southside Street | tel. 01752 665292 | plymouth gin.com)* has produced *Plymouth Gin* here since 1783. On the other side of the harbour, you can see a British and an American flag on Mayflower Steps, the jetty where settlers are said to have boarded the *Mayflower* in 1620 to seek a new life in America. You can learn more at the *Mayflower Museum (April–Oct Mon–Sat 9am–5pm, Sun 10am–4pm, Nov–March Mon–Fri 9am–5pm, Sat 10am–4pm | admission £5 | 3–5 The Barbican | mayflowermuseum. co.uk | 1 hr). d–e 5–6*

THE HOE

The limestone cliff is one of Plymouth's most impressive sights. There is a wonderful view of the harbour and sea from the clifftop, backed by a green. The landmark red-and-white lighthouse, *Smeaton's Tower (daily 10am–5pm | admission £5 | Hoe Road)*, has a fabulous clifftop position. In 1588, Sir Francis Drake is said to have played a game of bowls on the Hoe before he put to sea to defeat the Spanish Armada. A statue on the green immortalises the mariner. The *Royal Citadel* on the eastern end of the Hoe is still used for military purposes, but in summer you can join guided tours of the 17th-century fort *(April–Sept | admission £12.50 | advance booking required | english-heritage.org.uk).* ⊞ *c–d 5–6*

NATIONAL MARINE AQUARIUM ⚓

Great Britain's biggest aquarium also has the deepest tank in the country. It contains fish from the Atlantic and surrounding area and a special tropical tank with fish from warmer parts. *Daily 10am–5pm | admission £22.50 | Rope Walk | Coxside | national-aquarium. co.uk |* ⏲ *2 hrs |* ⊞ *e5*

ROYAL WILLIAM YARD

Former abattoirs and bakeries now house cafés and restaurants offering gastro food and trendy drinks and are mainly situated on the quayside. The largest military area in west Plymouth was once a victualling depot for the Royal Navy. Behind the impressive entrance gate is an entire district with renovated warehouses, businesses and retailers. For an idyllic way to enjoy dinner or drinks, take the boat and avoid the traffic while getting great views of the coast. A *ferry service (April–Oct daily 9.30am–5pm, Nov 11am–5.30pm | £4 per trip | plymouthboattrips.co.uk)* connects Royal William Yard with the Barbican district. ⊞ *0*

INSIDER TIP
Drinks ahoy!

EATING & DRINKING

BISTROT PIERRE

This French-style restaurant serves an excellent choice of Anglo-French cuisine: healthy dishes featuring plenty of fish, vegetables and meat options – accompanied by delicious wine. *New Cooperage, Royal William Yard | tel. 01752 262318 | short.travel/ cod9 | £££ |* ⊞ *0*

CROWN & ANCHOR

Classic pub fare from fish & chips to steak: this pub in the historic harbour district is always busy. Hearty food and reasonable prices – the best time to come is on Sundays for their roasts. *10 The Barbican | tel. 01752 224572 | £ |* ⊞ *e5*

KINGFISHER FISH & CHIPS

This fish and chip shop has been voted the best in the country several times. It doesn't have the biggest range of dishes and the atmosphere is what you would expect from any other such shop, but the quality of the food is outstanding. *Chaddlewood Shopping Centre, 6 Glen Road | tel. 01752 335567 | £ |* ⊞ *0*

SHOPPING

DRAKE CIRCUS ⚓

This shopping centre in town has 70 shops and is a great alternative to sightseeing on rainy days. Every chain store in the country seems to have a branch here. *1 Charles Street | drake circus.com |* ⊞ *d4*

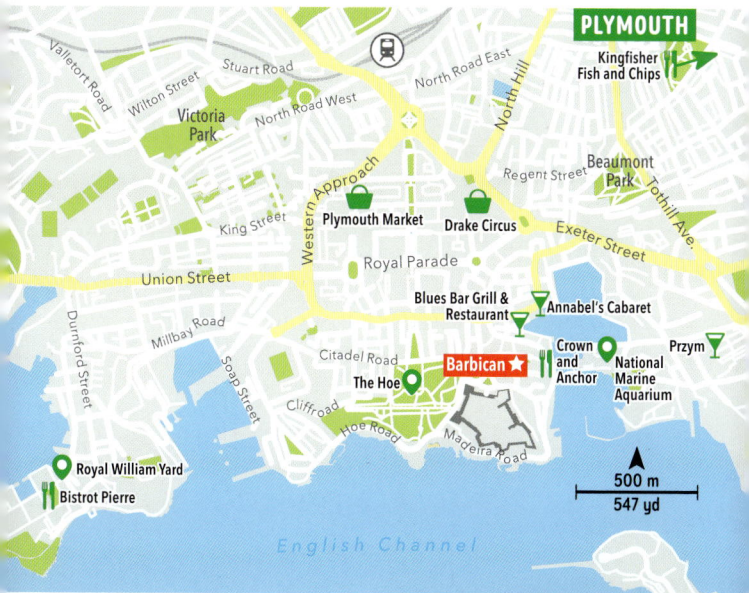

PLYMOUTH

Kingfisher
Fish and Chips

Plymouth Market
Drake Circus

Blues Bar Grill &
Restaurant
Annabel's Cabaret

Crown
and
Anchor
Przym

The Hoe
Barbican ★
National
Marine
Aquarium

Royal William Yard
Bistrot Pierre

English Channel

500 m
547 yd

PLYMOUTH MARKET

Great for browsing: the 150-odd stalls in Plymouth Market may offer more junk and bric-a-brac than real market goods, but you're guaranteed not to leave here without buying something. *Cornwall Street | plymouthmarket. co.uk |* 🗺 *c4*

SPORT & ACTIVITIES

TINSIDE LIDO

The Tinside Lido, built in 1935 in Art Deco style, is one of the most attractive open-air pools in the country and offers spectacular views over the sea and town. In summer, there is occasionally an open-air cinema here. *June–Sept Mon–Fri noon–6pm, Sat/ Sun 10am–6pm | admission £5.20 | Hoe Road |* 🗺 *c6*

NIGHTLIFE

ANNABEL'S CABARET

Lounge-style club in the harbour district with good cocktails and music that falls somewhere between blues, rock and pop. Regular live music and parties. *88 Vauxhall Street | tel. 01752 260555 | annabelscabaret.co.uk |* 🗺 *e5*

BLUES BAR GRILL & RESTAURANT

A popular spot for live music (blues, jazz) in the Barbican district. It also serves burgers and steaks to line your stomach. *8 The Parade | tel. 01752 257345 | bluesbarandgrill.co.uk |* 🗺 *d5*

AROUND PLYMOUTH

13 BUCKLAND ABBEY

15km / 20 mins north of Plymouth (by car)

The medieval abbey with its imposing nave would make the perfect backdrop for a religious crime thriller. Buckland Abbey was built in 1278 as a Cistercian abbey and, like all England's abbeys, was closed during Henry VIII's Dissolution of the Monasteries in the 16th century. In 1541, Sir Richard Grenville converted the abbey into a private residence and later sold it to the famous circumnavigator Sir Francis Drake. *Feb–Oct daily 11am–5pm, Nov Sat/Sun 11am–4pm, Dec daily 11am–4pm | Yelverton | nationaltrust.org.uk/buckland-abbey | admission £14 | ⊙ 2 hrs | ⊞ L8*

14 SALTRAM

8km / 15 mins east of Plymouth (by car)

The film of Jane Austen's novel *Sense and Sensibility* was filmed here in 1995. And this impressive country house in a wonderful parkland estate on the River Plym still feels like a film set. You can tour the luxuriously furnished rooms with Chinese wallpaper and many historic and valuable paintings. *Daily park 10am–4pm, house 11am–3.30pm | admission £13 | Plympton | nationaltrust.org.uk/saltram | ⊙ 1 hr | ⊞ L9*

15 BURGH ISLAND ★

35km / 45 mins east of Plymouth (by car)

Agatha Christie is said to have written *Evil under the Sun* in the Burgh Island Hotel. But you don't need to stay – the rugged, small tidal island is well worth a day visit. At low tide, it takes only a few minutes to walk from 🏖 *Bigbury Bay* – the sandy beach with a view of Burgh Island is perfect for relaxing – while at high tide you take a *Sea Tractor (£2, free for hotel guests)*. The island has rocky cliffs and the ruins of a small medieval chapel as well as the quaint *Pilchard Inn*, a very old guesthouse that would be the perfect place to film a pirate movie. Of course, you can also stopover at Burgh Island Hotel. ⊙ *3 hrs | ⊞ M9*

DARTMOOR

(⊞ L–N 6–8) **Sherlock Holmes was the famous detective of this region and Edgar Wallace made this the backdrop for his crime stories. Dartmoor ★, Devon's unique and in many parts isolated moorland, is almost made for detective thrillers.**

The place is full of narrow, single-track roads with few passing places that can make driving hazardous. However, the countryside, with its many impressive sights, is inviting for hikers and photographers. Tiny villages, like popular Widecombe-in-the-Moor, are hidden away, while imposing stone formations such as Hound Tor offer inspiration for new

At low tide you can walk across the sand to Burgh Island

stories. All the myths surrounding Dartmoor are fuelled by one thing in particular: a fear for one's life. But nowadays it's pretty safe and you've got nothing to fear. However, you should be aware that the British Army uses parts of the national park for military training. You can find information about when firing exercises will be taking place at *short.travel/cod1*.

SIGHTSEEING

CASTLE DROGO ☂

The last castle to be built in Britain is more modern than it first appears. Building work for this medieval-style castle only began in 1910 and continued until 1930. With its impressive location high above the Teign Valley, it is visible from a distance. The castle is fully furnished and artists have redesigned some of the rooms. Outside, you have a lovely view of the valley. *March–Oct daily 11am–5pm, Nov/Dec Sat/Sun 11am–4pm, grounds always open | admission £14 | Drewsteignton (near Exeter) | nationaltrust.org.uk/castle-drogo |* ⏱ *2 hrs*

MORETONHAMPSTEAD MOTOR MUSEUM

This museum is just the ticket for a rainy day. Located in an old bus depot, the museum features 150 British and international classic cars. Every petrol head's dream! *April–Oct Tue–Thu, Sat/Sun 11.30am–4.30pm | admission £8 | Court Street | Moretonhampstead | moretonmotormuseum.co.uk |* ⏱ *2 hrs*

Enjoy the spectacular rocky tors on Dartmoor

HOUND TOR

This cluster of stones doesn't seem like much from below, but when you reach the top, you'll have a spectacular view – and in the mornings in particular, when there isn't anyone else around, there is a kind of magical stillness. There are plenty of tales surrounding the eye-catching stone formations – the site of a former village – north of Widecombe. These have been joined by more recent stories of the filming of TV series *Sherlock*, with actor Benedict Cumberbatch. The unusual formation is said to be a pack of dogs that were turned to stone by witches. The 6m-high granite rock, known as *Bowerman's Nose (6km north)*, is reputed to be the hunter. *Free access*

WIDECOMBE-IN-THE-MOOR

This picturesque village (pop. 600) in the heart of Dartmoor, nestled among hills and moorland, emerged as a collection of small stone cottages around *St Pancras Church*. The writer Beatrice Chase is buried in the old cemetery. You can buy souvenirs at the *General Store*, formerly a brewery and later a school. *widecombe-in-the-moor.com*

LYDFORD GORGE

The gorge has carved its way 2.4km through woodlands in the heart of southwest England. You can explore it on a 5km circular trail, which is steep and narrow in certain parts. The highlight is *White Lady Waterfall*, which has a 30m drop where the River Burn cascades into the River Lyd. In May, a mass of bluebells transforms the gorge into a sea of blue. In *Lydford* village you can view the ruins of 🐾 *Lydford Castle (always open | free admission | english-heritage.org.uk). April–Sept daily 10am–4.30pm, Oct–Dec shorter hours | admission £11 | entrance at the west end of Lydford Village | nationaltrust.org.uk/lydford-gorge |* ⏱ *2 hrs*

EATING & DRINKING

CAFÉ ON THE GREEN

Ideal spot for lunch and afternoon tea. The large café in the centre of Widecombe can be a bit busy at times, but there is plenty of outside seating to enjoy al fresco dining in summer. *The Green, Widecombe-in-the-Moor | tel. 01364 621720 | thecafeonthe green.co.uk | £*

THE CLEAVE PUBLIC HOUSE

In this thatched pub in the middle of Dartmoor you can enjoy hearty British food from fish to steak as well as vegetarian options – all in the most idyllic surroundings. *Lustleigh | tel. 01647 277223 | thecleavelustleigh. co.uk | ££*

WELLNESS

BOVEY CASTLE

This hotel that resembles a castle offers one of the best spas in Devon – you can come here to indulge, even if you don't book a room. Relax with an amazing view, enjoy some treatments and take a dip in the pool. *North Bovey, Newton Abbot | tel. 01647 445000 | boveycastle.com/spa*

AROUND DARTMOOR

16 OKEHAMPTON

Directly northwest of the national park

The beautiful old houses give this small town (pop. 7,000) its picturesque appearance. Despite its diminutive size, it is somewhat of a hub on the edge of Dartmoor. On a wooded spur, the 11th-century ruins of *Okehampton Castle (April–Oct daily 10am–5pm | admission £5.90 | Castle Lodge | english-heritage. org.uk)* are well worth a visit. A wonderful cycle route on an old railway track, *Granite Way*, is mainly traffic free. It stretches from Okehampton railway station for 18km to Meldon Viaduct and gives spectacular views of the surrounding countryside *(bicycle hire: Granite Way Cycle Hire | Klondyke Road, Okehampton | tel. 01837 650907).* 📖 *L5*

INSIDER TIP
Cycle along the railway

NORTH DEVON

ENGLAND OF YESTERYEAR

You will have heard of Exmoor, but have you heard of Great Torrington, Lundy or Bideford? If not, you're not alone. North Devon is for connoisseurs: it has far fewer well-known spots than the south.

The areas here can be rugged, and you might feel as if you've stepped back in time. You will see dramatic rocky cliffs, attractive beaches and lots of surfing, as well as endless undulating countryside and mist-covered fields inland.

The remote green hillsides of North Devon

Rather like the rest of Devon, you might say. Well, almost, although the northern part is more remote, and in some areas you might not meet another soul. Here, you can discover all that the local landscape has to offer – including the ubiquitous Exmoor ponies and sheep. You can also visit the many villages where owner-run shops and craftspeople keep up some old English traditions. And don't forget the coast! The view over the Bristol Channel has seen many a visitor re-examine the priorities in their life.

25km, 2 hrs

p. 104
Ilfracombe

40km, 40 mins

5 Lundy Island ⭐

Verity ⭐

Woolacombe Beach **4** Woolacombe Bay

Georgeham

Croyde

Saunton

Knowle

Braunton

C E L T I C   S E A

Yelland

Westward Ho! Beach

Appledore

Westward Ho! **6**

Northam

39

The Big Sheep **7**

8 Bideford

Hartland Coast **10**   **9** Clovelly ⭐

Alverdiscott

386

Weare Giffard

Hartland

Great Torrington
p. 109

Welcombe

Langtree

Little
Torrington

DEVON

39

Bradworthy

Kilkhampton

CORNWALL

Holsworthy Beacon

Bude

Chilsworthy

Highampton

Holsworthy

▲
5 km
3.11 mi

★ **VALLEY OF THE ROCKS**
Impressive rocky cliffs form this valley in Exmoor. ➤ p. 102

★ **LYNTON/LYNMOUTH**
These two lovely towns are connected via a Victorian water-powered funicular. ➤ p. 102

★ **VERITY**
Damien Hirst's bronze statue on the pier at Ilfracombe caused a great furore when it was unveiled in 2012. ➤ p. 104

★ **LUNDY ISLAND**
Cliffs and sea views, puffins and lambs: all the ingredients for a relaxing day out. The island on an outcrop off North Devon is a paradise for nature fans. ➤ p. 106

★ **CLOVELLY**
A small fishing village in a romantic setting – and traffic-free. A steep cobbled street leads down to a tiny harbour. ➤ p. 110

Bristol Channel

30km, 35 mins

Valley of the Rocks ★   **Lynton/Lynmouth** ★

Combe Martin Beach

31km, 35 mins

Barbrook

Parracombe

39

Challacombe

3 Arlington Court

E
p. 102

x   m   o   o   r

Porlock

Minehead

Timberscombe

SOMERSET

Bratton Fleming

Simonsbath

Exford

Withypool

Winsford

Goodleigh

Brayford

Barnstaple
p. 107

Charles

Brompton Regis

396

North Molton

Dulverton

25km, 1 hr 20 mins

Filleigh

Stags Head

South Molton

Umberleigh

George Nympton

Atherington

Alswear

361

High Bickington

Meshaw

Exebridge

Bampton

Oakford Bridge

Rackenford

396

Beaford

Witheridge

Knightshayes 1

Coldharbour Mill 2

Dolton

Chulmleigh

Drayford

Wembworthy

Chawleigh

377

Lapford

Tiverton

Bickleigh

Cadbury

Iddesleigh

Winkleigh

Morchard Bishop

Monkokehampton

Hatherleigh

Copplestone

Sandford

Thorverton

Jacobstowe

North Tawton

Bow

Crediton

386

EXMOOR

(◫ M–O 1–2) **Exmoor is known for its narrow valleys, hidden-away villages and sprawling pastures leading abruptly to sheer cliffs.**

The mist often shrouds it all in a milky haze. The national park has beautiful, almost ghostly, scenery. Near the source of the River Exe is one of Britain's most spectacular moorlands. The area is well known for the oldest breed of ponies on the British Isles: the Exmoor pony. It also has plenty of small bilberry bushes growing on the open moorland. Only part of Exmoor is in Devon – the rest is in Somerset.

SIGHTSEEING

DUNSTER CASTLE

A picture-book castle with towers and battlements, Dunster Castle sits above the medieval village of *Dunster* (pop. 800). Inside, the Victorian furnishings make it obvious that the building is more modern than you might have thought. It was in fact built in the 19th century – but it doesn't matter, it's still mighty impressive. The parkland setting is wonderful too and a narrow footpath leads to a watermill with a romantic café. *Castle March–Oct daily 10am–4pm, Nov/Dec Sat/Sun 10am–3pm, Park March–Oct daily 10am–6pm, rest of the year until 5pm | admission £16 | nationaltrust.org.uk/dunster-castle | ⏱ 2 hrs*

PORLOCK

This enchanted village (pop. 1,400) in the north of Exmoor looks like a picture postcard. The high street winds its way through the village and is also one of the central arteries crossing Exmoor from west to east. The aroma of coffee is in the air because *DJ Miles (The Vale Yard, High Street)*, a fine coffee roastery, was established here and produces excellent blends. The harbour off *Porlock Weir* is also lovely, with a slightly eerie feeling about it. Enjoy the peace and quiet by the water and go for a pint at the *Bottom Ship (£)*, a centuries-old pub with a thatched roof by the harbour.

INSIDER TIP Top beans

VALLEY OF THE ROCKS ★

Don't be alarmed if a goat crosses your path here. On the coast between Lynton and Porlock, nature has created a unique and scenic location with impressive, rocky hills that are partly overgrown with grass. Feral goats live here and obviously enjoy the fabulous views. You should join them!

LYNTON/LYNMOUTH ★

Two towns for the price of one: while Lynton sits proudly on the clifftops of Exmoor, down below Lynmouth has developed into a sleepy seaside village. The two places are linked by the water-powered *Cliff Railway (daily 10am–7pm in the summer, otherwise until 5pm | one-way ticket £3.50 | The Esplanade, Lynmouth | tel. 01598 753908 | cliffrailwaylynton.co.uk)*, a funicular which takes visitors back to the 19th century: the tank of a carriage is filled with water until it is heavy enough to descend into the valley. It has operated on the same principle since 1890. There is a spectacular view at the top from the tiny *Cliff Top Café (Lee Road | tel. 01598 75 33 66 | £)*.

EATING & DRINKING

THE CASTLE 🚩

This pleasant pub in a Tudor house is in the centre of Porlock. Here you can get hearty English food from morning untill night, including fish and chips, sandwiches and soups. *High Street, Porlock | tel. 01643 862504 | ££*

THE RISING SUN

The rustic exterior of this thatched house by the harbour is deceptive: this pub serves fine cuisine with freshly caught fish, seafood and other local products. *Lynmouth Street, Harbourside, Lynmouth | tel. 01598 753223 | risingsunlynmouth.co.uk | £££*

SPORT & ACTIVITIES

The best spots for surfing in North Devon are further west at Croyde, Woolacombe and Saunton. But *Exmoor Adventures (exmooradventures.co.uk)* offers a range of outdoor activities from Porlock Weir, including coasteering, climbing and kayaking. You can also rent bikes *(from £27 per day)*.

BEACHES

Exmoor has a variety of beaches. The most famous is *Minehead Beach* in the east (just across the border in Somerset), but pebbly *Porlock Beach*

Beneath the clouds, Exmoor shows off its magical side

and *Dunster Beach* are also worth a visit. If you're looking for a tiny, sandy bay, head to 🐾 *Combe Martin Beach*. Make sure you check the tide times (*tidetimes.org.uk*)!

AROUND EXMOOR

1 KNIGHTSHAYES

30km / 30 mins from Exmoor (via the A361 or A390)

A grand Victorian country mansion, Knightshayes looks like a great monastery, but it was never more than a private home. The eccentric architect and designer William Burges gave the rooms mainly dark, Gothic-revival decor – but perhaps they just look that way because he was fired before the building was finished. The house is surrounded by one of Devon's most attractive gardens. *March–Oct daily 10am–5pm, Nov–Feb garden daily, house only Sat/Sun 10am–4pm | admission £14 | Bolham, Tiverton | nationaltrust.org.uk/knightshayes |* ⏱ *2 hrs |* 🗺 *O4*

INSIDER TIP
As green as it gets

2 COLDHARBOUR MILL 🐾

35km / 35 mins from Exmoor (via the A396 and A361)

This old wool factory takes you back to Victorian times. The guided tour will explain all the machinery that still fills the production halls. Children can go on a scavenger hunt to discover how yarn was spun. *April–Oct Wed–Sat 10.30am–4.30pm, Jan–March Thu 11am–3.30pm | admission £15, children £8 | Uffculme, Cullompton | coldharbourmill.org.uk |* ⏱ *2 hrs |* 🗺 *P4*

ILFRACOMBE

(🗺 *L1*) **Back in the 19th century, secluded Ilfracombe (pop. 12,000) tried to achieve a balance between the harbour and seaside resort. Today, it is primarily a lovely, somewhat antiquated, holiday destination.**

The centre still showcases elegant Victorian architecture, even if the paint is peeling here and there. While no longer a popular bathing resort, the town retains a maritime flair that is unrivalled in this area. Ilfracombe has survived as a sleepy town with small boats in the harbour and the unmistakable feeling that everyone here has all the time in the world.

SIGHTSEEING

VERITY ⭐

In an authentic harbour town like Ilfracombe, you don't exactly expect world-class art – so, Damien Hirst's bronze statue *Verity* gets even more attention than it would elsewhere. It has stood on the pier at the entrance to the harbour since 2012. Highly controversial at first, the statue shows a 20m-tall pregnant woman with raised sword and open womb revealing the

On the pier at Ilfracombe: *Verity* by Damien Hirst

foetus and organs inside. It caused a great furore in the press across the country; the town was unaccustomed to so much attention. But critics now accept that the scandalous lady enhances the location. *Harbour Front*

ST NICHOLAS CHAPEL

The small chapel on the green at Lantern Hill by the harbourside was for centuries a destination for pilgrims. In the medieval period, it was used as a lighthouse. The steep uphill path is well worth the climb: you have a fabulous view of the village from here. *Daily May–Sept 10am–6pm, April and Oct 10am–4pm | free admission | Lantern Hill*

LANDMARK THEATRE

It is already eye-catching from the promenade: two large cones seem to be propped on top of the flat building. Some people think it looks like a nuclear power plant; in Ilfracombe the locals refer to the controversial building as "Madonna's bra" – for obvious reasons. The theatre is run by a British touring theatre company, and it features a constantly changing programme. *Wilder Road*

EATING & DRINKING

THE PIER

This pub is in a prime location. You sit right beside the harbour, sampling all kinds of beers and enjoying pub food such as burgers or fish and chips. *The Quay | tel. 01271 865516 | ££*

SWISS COTTAGE CAFÉ

This café in the town centre may not look very Swiss, but it serves exquisite cakes from its own bakery. It also sells freshly roasted coffee. *33 High Street | swisscottagecafe.com | £*

BEACHES

The beach in Ilfracombe is called *Tunnels Beaches*. For a bigger but busier beach, head to *Woolacombe Beach* about 10km to the west.

AROUND ILFRACOMBE

3 ARLINGTON COURT

20km / 25 mins southwest of Ilfracombe (via the A3123)

The Regency country house looks as though it was recently vacated.

Flowers bloom by the entrance, while inside there is an exhibition about everyday life in the 19th century. In the adjoining barn, the *National Carriage Museum* displays about 40 horse-drawn vehicles from different eras. The garden is spectacular. *March–Oct daily 10am–4pm (house 11am–3.30pm), Nov/Dec and Feb Sat/Sun 10am–4pm | admission £14 | Arlington | nationaltrust.org.uk | ⏱ 2 hrs | ⊞ L2*

4 WOOLACOMBE BAY

11km / 15 mins west of Ilfracombe (via the B3343)

Woolacombe's sweeping sandy beach is one of the finest in Devon – there are always quiet little spots to be found along the 5km of coast. It's perfect for surfing! And when it's raining, why not have a creative afternoon at the *Craft Hut (Feb–Oct daily 10am–5pm | Sandy Lane, Woolacombe Bay Holiday Park | tel. 01271 872536)*: children can paint pottery animals, cups or dinosaurs, which you pick up the following day after they've been fired. ⊞ K1

INSIDER TIP Creative kids

5 LUNDY ISLAND ★

25km / 2 hrs west of Ilfracombe (by ferry)

This is the perfect spot for guaranteed relaxation: Lundy is a small island in the Bristol Channel. It is not always accessible, even in the summer, and takes two hours to reach on a return boat trip. On the island there are impressive rocky outcrops and wild countryside – as well as a few houses, a lighthouse and the medieval small

Marisco Castle. Otherwise, there are mainly sheep, puffins and tremendous sea views from almost every point. The Landmark Trust has converted some of the beautiful, old sandstone buildings into visitor accommodation so you can stay overnight. In the summer months, there are day trips with the *MS Oldenburg* (April–Oct approx. every other day | day trip £50, return £89), depending on tides, from Bideford or Ilfracombe. In winter, on specific dates there is a *helicopter (from Hartland Point | £158 return)*. *Lundy Shore Office, The Quay, Bideford | tel. 01271 863636 | landmarktrust. org.uk/lundyisland)* | 🗺 G1

INSIDER TIP
Trip to see the puffins

BARNSTAPLE

(🗺 L2) **The town centre of Barnstaple (pop. 24,000) is bustling all day.**

People come from the surrounding area to do their shopping here. This is the place in North Devon where people go about their daily business, see friends and get noticed. There are numerous stores around the old Pannier Market, most of them hip delicatessens and takeaway coffee shops.

SIGHTSEEING

MUSEUM OF BARNSTAPLE & NORTH DEVON
The perfect introduction to the history of North Devon. There are displays showing the development of Barnstaple and the local region – from 11th-century coins to shipwrecks from the 17th century. In front of the museum is the *Albert Clock Tower*, a memorial to Queen Victoria's Prince Consort and husband, Albert of Saxe-Coburg and Gotha, unveiled in 1862. *March–Oct Mon–Sat 10am–5pm, Nov–Feb 10am–4pm | free admission | The Square | barnstaplemuseum.org.uk |* ⏱ *1 hr*

EATING & DRINKING

ALEXANDER'S SANDWICH BAR
The sandwich was invented in England, and in this sandwich shop, you'll find some of the best: the freshly prepared sarnies – made with tuna, ham, cheese and more – surpass any pre-packaged version. *31C Boutport Street | tel. 01271 373735 | £*

Herring gull and sea thrift on Lundy Island

foods here, from jams to organic sausages, on Tuesdays, Fridays and Saturdays. *Mon–Sat 9am–3pm | Butchers Row*

AROUND BARNSTAPLE

6 WESTWARD HO!

17km / 20 mins west of Barnstaple (via the A39)

The seaside resort Westward Ho! (pop. 2,000) is mainly famous for its punctuation – it is the only placename in Europe that officially ends with an exclamation mark. The name is based on the novel by Charles Kingsley who persuaded investors to build the town. But tourists are usually here just for the popular 🏖 sandy beach. Nearby is *Appledore*, a romantic fishing village that continues to thrive, thanks to its shipyard. *K3*

7 THE BIG SHEEP

18km / 20 mins west of Barnstaple (via the A39)

Once this was an ordinary farm; now it is a large family theme park focused on rural life and animals. The sheep are still the stars but the attractions also feature other animals, such as swan pedalos, a piggy pull-along ride and much more. There are also live animals (including lambs) for petting, admiring and taking selfies! Grownups can visit the brewery and gin distillery on site. *April–Oct daily 10–5pm | admission £16.95 in*

You can cycle or hike along the Tarka Trail

BLOCK

A culinary world tour in miniature: at this sought-after restaurant in the town centre, you can get ramen noodles, miso cheeseburgers or burrito bowls. Sound confusing? It's actually an exciting concept and the food is delicious. *12–14 Butchers Row | tel. 01271 342045 | eatatblock.com | ££*

SHOPPING

PANNIER MARKET

Barnstaple's market hall was a model for many others in Devon. Since the mid-19th century, market traders have offered their merchandise here. Nowadays, the Pannier Market has more or less become a permanent flea market. But you can still buy local *summer, £5.50 in winter | Abbotsham (near Bideford) | thebigsheep.co.uk | ▥ K3*

TARKA TRAIL

The Tarka Trail, about 290km, is traffic free and goes through beautiful countryside. You can explore the trail on foot or by bicycle. From Barnstaple it follows a circular route via Braunton, Ilfracombe and Lynton and back. About 50km of the route travels along a disued railway track. The trail is named after *Tarka the Otter*, a novel by Henry Williamson. You can hire bicycles from *Tarka Bikes (The Railway Station, Barnstaple | tel. 01271 324202 | tarkabikes.co.uk).* ▥ L-M 1-2

GREAT TORRINGTON

(▥ K3) **Great Torrington (pop. 6,000) seems rather inconspicuous, but the small town offers more than you may think at a first glance.**

The town centre has many medieval buildings. A quick tour of one of the side streets or the car park at the Pannier Market will quickly lead you to the countryside, since Great Torrington is set in one of North Devon's most attractive rural locations.

SIGHTSEEING

ROSEMOOR

It's all in the name: about 2,000 roses and 200 different varieties grow in this garden outside Great Torrington, which is more of a park than a simple garden. At Christmas, the trees are lit up with colourful illuminations at twilight. *Daily April-Sept 10am-6pm, Oct-March 10am-5pm | admission £13.85 | A3124 | rhs.org.uk/gardens/rosemoor*

EATING & DRINKING

THE TORRIDGE INN

An unusual combination: Thai food is prepared in this rustic pub – curries, noodle dishes and more. *136 Mill Street, Taddiport | tel. 01805 625042 | ££*

SHOPPING

PANNIER MARKET

The small market hall has different offers every day and was formerly the trading hub of Great Torrington. Now it sells everyday items and is a food market from Thursday to Saturday. *Mon-Sat 7am-6pm | South Street*

AROUND GREAT TORRINGTON

🔳 BIDEFORD

12km / 13 mins north of Great Torrington (via the A386)

Bideford (pop. 17,000) is well known for its lovely old round-arched *Long Bridge* over the River Torridge.

Cobblestones and cottages on the steep coast in picturesque Clovelly

Measuring 200m in length, it is one of the longest bridges of its kind in England. But visitors to the town are usually here for one reason: shopping. Bideford has a typical market hall with a weekly market on Tuesdays and Saturdays. Otherwise, the shops are mainly galleries and souvenir stores. If you head west out of Bideford, you will find the outlet mall 🕇 *Affinity Devon (Mon–Wed, Fri/Sat 9am–6pm, Thu 9am–8pm, Sun 10am–4pm)* on Clovelly Road. **INSIDER TIP** **Bag a bargain** Here, you can shop for around 35 brands ranging from fashion to perfume, with plenty of special offers. *K3*

🟪 CLOVELLY ⭐

30km / 30 mins west of Great Torrington (via the A39)

The privately owned village of Clovelly is traffic-free and even pedestrians have to pay to enter. But this helps make it one of North Devon's most attractive destinations. Small cottages line the steep cobblestone road down to the harbour. This is a picture-postcard setting and the harbour is romantic, which makes it something of a tourist hotspot. The writer Charles Kingsley was born here. He immortalised Clovelly in his book *Westward Ho!* in which the character Salvation Yeo was born in what is currently the *Red Lion Hotel (The Quay | tel. 01237 431237 | ££)*. You can still enjoy a meal here with a view of the tiny

harbour. *Daily 9am–6pm | admission £8.50 | clovelly.co.uk |* ⏱ *3 hrs |* 📖 *J3*

⑩ HARTLAND COAST

35km / 45 mins west of Great Torrington (via the A39)

The *Hartland Point Lighthouse* marks the area where the Bristol Channel flows into the Atlantic. The weather at the top is often bitterly cold and windy. It's a lonely place, but that's what makes this region of North Devon so magical. Severe storms gradually destroyed the once-busy port at *Hartland Quay*; parts of the old quay wall are still visible at low tide. The simple *Hartland Quay Hotel (Hartland, Bideford | tel. 01237 441218 | hartland quayhotel.co.uk | ££)* offers fabulous views and a small local history *museum (Easter–mid-Oct daily 11am–4pm | admission £1).* Grab yourself a tea or beer at the bar or, in fine weather, sit outside with a view of the sea. *Hartland Abbey* is now a country house with lovely gardens *(April–Sept Sun–Thu 11am–5pm, house 2–5pm | admission £15.50 | Hartland).* 📖 *H3*

ON THE TRAIL OF SMUGGLERS

Devon and Cornwall have many hiking trails along wonderful unspoiled routes. The 🚩 *South West Coast Path (southwestcoastpath.org. uk)* is one of the highlights. The trail covers 1,014km along the coasts of both counties and beyond. It begins at Minehead in Somerset on the edge of Exmoor and ends near Poole Harbour, in Dorset, Devon's neighbouring county. The best features are the perfect sea views, the clifftops, secluded cabins and small villages.

Originally the path – which follows the entire coastline – was not a hiking route but was used by coastguards to stop smugglers moving quickly from one location to another. If the whole trail sounds like too much of a trek, you can pick a stretch – even a small section will be a memorable experience. Simply follow the symbols along the route – a white acorn on a brown background (and keep the sea on your right!).

DISCOVERY TOURS

Want to get under the skin of this region? Then our discovery tours are the ideal guide – they provide advice on which sights to visit, tips on where to stop for that perfect holiday snap, a choice of the best places to eat and drink, and suggestions for fun activities.

❶ ON THE TRAIL OF AGATHA CHRISTIE

➤ Visit the childhood haunts of the Queen of Crime
➤ Explore the famous author's summer residence
➤ Trundle along the coast on an old steam train

📍 Torquay Museum, Torquay

🏁 Grand Hotel, Torquay

➡ 5.5km, plus journey to Greenway

🚶 1 day (total driving time 1½ hrs)

ℹ Check the timetable for Dartmouth Steam Railway (dartmouthrailriver.co.uk). You must let the conductor know that you are getting off at Greenway.

The grand master of English crime writing: Dame Agatha Christie

HARBOUR VIEWS AND POISONOUS PLANTS

Start at the **❶ Torquay Museum** *(Tue–Thu and Sat 10am–4pm | 529 Babbacombe Road | torquaymuseum. org)* which has a small section dedicated to Agatha Christie. *Via Parkhill Road* you arrive at **❷ The Imperial Hotel** ➤ **p. 86** where Christie supposedly enjoyed afternoon tea. The hotel is featured in several of her novels. While sipping a cup of tea in the **restaurant** you can enjoy the view over Torquay. *On the way to the harbour,* you will pass **❸ Beacon Cove** where, like Agatha Christie, you can paddle in the water. *Stroll onwards to the* **❹ harbour**, where many buildings date from the writer's era. Order a coffee and sandwich in one of the cafés. Relax and enjoy the views of the boats! *Behind the Tourist Information Office at Cary Parade* is a **❺ bronze bust** of Agatha Christie. In the **❻ Pavilion**, Agatha and Archie Christie once listened to a Wagner concert – the date culminated in a marriage proposal.

Now, walk to the **❼ Princess Gardens**, which feature in *The ABC Murders;* the detour is worth it to see the exotic plants. *Immediately opposite, at* **❽ Princess Pier**, Christie used to go roller skating. Enjoy a stroll to the end of the pier. In the garden of **❾ Torre Abbey** ➤ **p. 85**

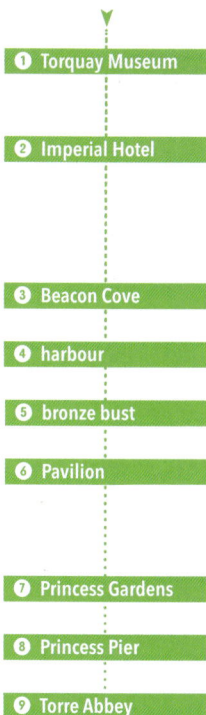

❶ Torquay Museum
❷ Imperial Hotel
❸ Beacon Cove
❹ harbour
❺ bronze bust
❻ Pavilion
❼ Princess Gardens
❽ Princess Pier
❾ Torre Abbey

there is a special area dedicated to poisonous plants: murder (for Agatha Christie) can be so easy and many of the victims in her books were killed with the poisons from exotic plants. *From the nearby ⑩ train station at Torquay, continue to the neighbouring town of* **Paignton ➤ p. 87**.

TO THE SUMMER HOUSE AND BACK

Take the Dartmouth Steam Railway and travel just as they did in Miss Marple's day *from Paignton to* **⑪ Greenway ➤ p. 89**. *A bus takes you from the train station to the country estate.* Welcome to the home of Agatha Christie! For many years Greenway was her summer residence. You can admire the house as well as many of her personal items – the view from the gardens across the River Dart is fantastic. Before you leave, you should enjoy a cider or cream tea at the small **Barn Café**. The shop also sells some of Christie's books.

At 4pm, *head by boat to* **Dartmouth ➤ p. 88**. Here, you must *cross to the other side at* **Kingswear ➤ p. 88** to catch the last *steam train back to Paignton* at 5pm. From here, you can take the *train back to* **Torquay**. Feeling tired from your exertions? *Immediately opposite the station* you will see the **⑫ Grand Hotel** *(Torbay Road | tel. 01803 296677 | grandtorquay.co.uk | £££)*. During

dinner, you can enjoy the view of the bay of Torbay and imagine how it must have been to be Agatha Christie: the doyenne of crime spent a night in this hotel on her honeymoon in 1914.

② HIKING ON THE SOUTH WEST COAST PATH

➤ Hike with the best views
➤ Lunch at a beach restaurant
➤ Enjoy the sea and the cliffs

📍 Newquay bus station

🏁 Great Western Hotel, Newquay

→ 15km, plus bus ride from Newquay

🥾 1 day (total walking time 4½ hrs)

ℹ Bus 56 from ❶ Newquay bus station: please check the timetable (firstgroup.com/cornwall), buses only run once an hour. ❸ Bedruthan Steps: please be aware of the strong surf here; the bay is only accessible at low tide. The steps are closed in winter.

COASTAL VIBES WITH TEA BREAK

From the **❶ bus station** in **Newquay ➤ p.57**, *hop on the 56 bus to start the hiking tour. Get off at Porthcothan Bay. At the red telephone box carry on along the path in the direction of Stores.* Now you are on the South West Coast Path – the symbol for the trail is a white acorn on a brown background.

Continue towards the coast: the romantically rugged coastline at **❷ Porthcothan Bay** is your first photo stop. *Keep heading southwest,* with the sea always on your right-hand side. Close to the path you will notice six burial barrows, which date from the Bronze Age. You can also find unusual plants such as the Cornish mallow with pink flowers, yellow flowering golden samphire and pink beach lilac. They light up this part of the coast with their vibrant colours, depending on the time of year. *Carry on, always following the coastline. Before the bay at Park Head* the free-standing rocks of **❸ Bedruthan Steps ➤ p.59** seem to emerge from the rugged coastline. In summer, a narrow path leads down to the beach. *At the National Trust car park for* **❹ Carnewas Island** *there is time to stop at the café (March–Oct daily) to enjoy a nice cup of tea! Head back to the coast path and continue in a southwesterly direction; enjoy the view between the rocky coastline and green countryside inland. At* **❺ Mawgan Porth** you will notice the first surfer crowds.

LUNCH, SEA VIEWS AND A LOVELY TERRACE

It's time for lunch. In **❻ Watergate Bay** you can stop at **The Beach Hut ➤ p.58** and enjoy the romantic view across the bay. If possible, try and get a table right by the window so you can lose yourself in those beautiful views. Afterwards, you can have a dip in the sea to wake yourself up again.

❶ bus station	
14km 20 mins	
❷ Porthcothan Bay	
4km 1 hr	
❸ Bedruthan Steps	
1km 10 mins	
❹ Carnewas Island	
2km 40 mins	
❺ Mawgan Porth	
3km 45 mins	
❻ Watergate Bay	

Continue on the South West Coast Path. The area is starting to get busier. In the distance, you can see the outskirts of Newquay. Don't miss the opportunity for a last glance at the natural rocky coastline – in Newquay the views are blocked by buildings. At Porth Beach in Newquay the coast path joins normal roads along some sections. *Continue towards the train station. Shortly before you reach it, turn left where Narrowcliff turns into Cliff Road* and you will see the ❼ **Great Western Hotel** *(Cliff Road | greatwesternnewquay. co.uk).* Behind the hotel (just go through the building) there is a terrace with a fabulous view over Great Western Beach – it's the perfect spot to relax with a Pimms and lemonade!

INSIDER TIP
Oh, summertime!

5km	1 ½ hrs

❼ Great Western Hotel

❸ CASTLES AND GARDENS

➤ **Discover palatial mansions**
➤ **Indulge in a cream tea while enjoying the gardens**
➤ **Relax in the spa at Bovey Castle**

📍 Lost Gardens of Heligan

🏁 Bovey Castle

➡ Approx. 240km

🚗 2 days (total driving time 4 hrs)

ℹ Some houses and gardens are closed in winter. Several houses and gardens are owned by the National Trust, and you can save on the admission fee with a Touring Pass *(nationaltrust.org.uk).*

GREENHOUSES AND JUNGLE
Start in the magnificent ❶ **Lost Gardens of Heligan** ➤ **p. 43**, recently restored but dating back to the 18th century. Explore the glasshouses and the jungle with its many subtropical plants! Carry on *via the B3287 and A390 to* ❷ **Trerice** ➤ **p. 58**, a typical

DAY 1
❶ Lost Gardens of Heligan

29km	30 mins

❷ Trerice

Elizabethan manor house. The Dutch gable façade is very unusual. After a tour of the building, you can enjoy lunch in the Barn Restaurant. Browse in the shop where you can also buy garden plants to take home.

FROM MANOR HOUSE TO CASTLE HOTEL

Head onto the A3058 and drive to the A30 to travel east. ❸ Lanhydrock ➤ p.69 is a country house that was originally a monastery. It is surrounded by a magnificent garden and large park. A tour of the house explains how the staff and owners lived in the past. In the shop, you can buy delicious shortbread from Cornwall to enjoy on the road! *Via the A39 continue to* ❹ Tintagel ➤ p.74, which is famous for its connection to the legend of King Arthur. In the Camelot Castle Hotel *(64 rooms | Atlantic Road | tel. 01840 770202 | camelotcastle.com),* you can spend the night by the coast. Relax and feel like a lord over dinner.

PICNIC AT KING ARTHUR'S CASTLE AND COUNTRY HOUSE CREAM TEAS

Early next morning set off in the car to *the ruins of* Tintagel Castle. On the way, you can stop and stock up with fresh caffè latte and Danish pastries at the Cornish Bakery – perfect for a picnic at the castle with sea views!

Then, *via the A395 continue to the A30 and onwards to the A388 to* ❺ Cotehele House *(daily 11am–4.30pm | St Dominick, Saltash | nationaltrust.org.uk/cotehele).* This is considered one of the most unspoiled examples of a example of Tudor-style country house. It is in a romantic setting high above the Tamar river and the garden is a show of colourful flowers depending on the season. Enjoy lunch by the river at Edgcumbe Tea Room. *Via the A388 and A38 it is not far to* ❻ Antony *(May–Sept Tue–Sun 12.30–4.30pm | Torpoint | nationaltrust.org.uk/antony).* The country house is famous for its portrait collection and the modern sculpture garden. After a tour, you can relax and enjoy a cream tea in the café.

❸ Lanhydrock

34km 35 mins
❹ Tintagel

DAY 2

60km 50 mins
❺ Cotehele House

34km 30 mins
❻ Antony

ACROSS DARTMOOR AND INTO THE SPA

Now it's time to set off for your overnight accommodation. *Carry on along the A386 and B3212 across Dartmoor.* Enjoy the scenic countryside on both sides of the route until you arrive in the northwest at ❼ **Bovey Castle ➤ p. 97**, an exclusive golf hotel in a former country house. Here, you can relax from your sightseeing tour in the swimming pool and enjoy some pampering in the spa.

51km 1 hr

❼ **Bovey Castle**

Cotehele House

PETS

Devon and Cornwall are animal friendly. Dogs are permitted to travel to Great Britain from an EU country if they have a microchip and domestic pet passport and have been vaccinated against rabies. They must also visit a vet one to five days before travel for worming treatment. Ferries make a small extra charge for dogs, which must remain in the car during the crossing.

CLIMATE & WHEN TO GO

Devon and Cornwall have a mild climate. It usually remains above freezing even in winter, and it almost never snows. In summer, temperatures can reach an average of 27°C. It does rain, but mostly in the form of showers rather than continuous rainfall.

GETTING AROUND

CAR

Driving in England is easier than it seems – especially if you stick to the left lane (overtake on the right). There are plenty of traffic lights, "give way" signs and roundabouts. You should give way to traffic already on the roundabout.

The speed limit is given in miles per hour. The maximum speed in built-up areas is generally 30mph/48kmh, except on single-carriage country roads where it is 60mph/96kmh, and on dual carriageways and motorways it is 70mph/112kmh. Vehicle licence plates are now scanned to check for speeding over longer distances. The blood alcohol limit is 0.5, and it is mandatory to wear a seatbelt for all passengers. Use of a mobile phone is also banned when driving, as well as driving cars in bus lanes. There are heavy fines for violating these laws.

Only park in designated parking spots. A solid line at the side of the road means no parking or waiting at certain times, while a double line means no stopping at any time. Parking illegally can cost you, and lots of local authorities use wheel clamps, which you can only unlock by fulfilling certain conditions. Many car parks have number plate recognition – even if there are no barriers, you still have to pay; otherwise, you may receive a penalty notice in the post.

More and more local authorities in bigger cities in the UK are implementing low-emission zones. You need to register your number plate in advance, and there are often strict emissions parameters. This does not apply to Devon and Cornwall yet, but you might encounter one of these zones on your way there, such as in London or Bristol.

CAR HIRE

The major international car hire firms are in Exeter and Plymouth. Prices are competitive, and it's advisable to book early to get a better deal. Search engines such as Check24 often have good deals.

PUBLIC TRANSPORT

The main railway line from London to Penzance stops at stations including

FESTIVALS & EVENTS
ALL YEAR ROUND

JANUARY
Winter at Eden: in January, the Eden Project organises special events – including an ice rink. *edenproject.com*

FEBRUARY
St Ives Feast: once a year, St Ives revives the old tradition of *Hurling the Silver Ball*, an early version of rugby.

MARCH
St Piran's Day *(photo)*: on or near 5 March, Cornwall remembers St Piran, the patron saint of the county. There are parades in Falmouth and Bodmin, among other events. *short.travel/cod12*

APRIL
Porthleven Food and Music Festival: *porthlevenfoodfestival.com*

MAY
Fowey Festival of Arts and Literature: *foweyfestival.com*

JULY
Looe Carnival: Looe celebrates carnival for an entire week in summer. *looelions.co.uk/carnival-week*

AUGUST
Regattas: major sailing competitions take place in Fowey, Torbay, Dartmouth, Salcombe and other places.

SEPTEMBER
Agatha Christie Festival *(Torquay)*: literature festival. *iacf-uk.org*

OCTOBER
Two Moors Festival *(Exmoor, Dartmoor)*: major festival of classical music. *twomoorsfestival.co.uk*

NOVEMBER
Ilfracombe Legends of Rock: music festival with many independent bands. *ilfracomberocksfestivals.co.uk*

DECEMBER
Padstow Christmas Festival: *padstow christmasfestival.co.uk*

Exeter, Plymouth and Truro. From the main line, branch lines lead to some coastal destinations. There are also a few cross-country *National Express* buses – otherwise the only options are regional bus routes, whose services are often infrequent, especially at weekends. The easiest way to get around is by car.

TAXI
Taxi fares are expensive. It is best to phone for a cab. Taxi ranks outside larger cities are rare.

HEALTH
The National Health Service (NHS) treats UK residents. Visitors from EU countries can access services with a European Health Insurance Card (EHIC). The EHIC is not an alternative to travel insurance; it will not cover any private medical healthcare, being flown back home, or lost or stolen property.

There are several national pharmacy chains (such as Boots, Lloyds and Superdrug) and pharmacies are also found in some large supermarkets.

EMERGENCIES

EMBASSIES & CONSULATES
EMBASSY OF IRELAND
17 Grosvenor Place, Belgravia, London SW1X 7HR | dfa.ie/irish-embassy/great-britain | tel. 020 7235 2171

HIGH COMMISSION OF AUSTRALIA
Strand, London WC2B 4LA | uk. embassy.gov.au | tel. 020 7379 4334

HIGH COMMISSION OF CANADA
Canada House, Trafalgar Square, London SW1Y 5BJ | canadainternational.gc.ca | tel. 0207 004 6000

US EMBASSY
33 Nine Elms Lane, London SW11 7US | uk.usembassy.gov | tel. 020 7499 9000

EMERGENCY SERVICES
Dial *999* or *112*

ESSENTIALS

ACCOMMODATION
British hotels once had a poor reputation, but now some of the grand old hotels have dusted themselves off to become chic boutique establishments and more and more decent budget hotels are opening.

Or there are *B&Bs* charging roughly £40 per person. B&B means literally a bed and breakfast – you usually avoid staying in the room during the daytime and allow your hosts some privacy.

There are also entire holiday apartment complexes offering more and more luxurious accommodation, which is also available for daily or weekly rates. The major providers are *Holiday Lettings (holidaylettings. co.uk)*, *Hoseasons (hoseasons.co.uk)* and *Airbnb (airbnb.com)*.

A pleasant alternative is the National Trust *(tel. 0344 8 00 20 70 (*)*

| nationaltrustholidays.org.uk), which rents out rooms and holiday apartments or even entire cottages on some of its country estates. The same applies for the *Landmark Trust (tel. 01628 825925 | landmarktrust.org.uk)*, which specialises in the rental of listed monuments, including lighthouses.

Youth hostels now offer double rooms as well as dormitories. The official body is the *Youth Hostel Association (tel. 01629 592700 | yha. org.uk)*. In some holiday locations there are also private hostels catering for young people.

Wild camping is not allowed in England, although it is often tolerated if you clear everything away. There are official campsites everywhere, and some have restaurants and high-quality washrooms (tourist information offices offer plenty of advice as well as the *Camping & Caravanning Club, campingandcaravanningclub. co.uk*). New campsites with large, stylish tents have cropped up recently, and some of them even have yurts or little cabins with jacuzzis or showers.

CUSTOMS

You can bring goods into the UK up to a value of £390, as well as large quantities of alcohol (42 litres of wine, 18 litres of beer and 4 litres of spirits). For information check: *gov.uk/browse/ abroad/travel-abroad*

ENTRANCE FEES

If you plan to visit the many historic sights, you can buy a weekly or annual pass for one of the major heritage organisations. *English Heritage*

HOW MUCH DOES IT COST?

Cappuccino	*about £3.20 for a mug in a coffee shop*
Sandwich	*about £3.50 in the supermarket*
Beer	*about £5.50 for a pint (568ml) in a pub*
Souvenir	*about £8 for a printed coffee mug*
Petrol	*about £1.45 for 1 litre*
Parking	*about £2.10 for 1 hour in a car park*

(annual membership £66 | english-heritage.org.uk) and the *National Trust (annual membership £76.80 | national trust.org.uk)* manage hundreds of country houses, palaces, several pubs and entire villages. Both also offer special passes online for one or two weeks (£37 and £45 respectively). The national parks have developed special tours where local people show visitors around, under the name *English National Park Experience Collection (nationalpark experiences.co.uk/home)*. Please note: Many attractions also offer admission with an additional donation, which obviously makes it more expensive.

INSIDER TIP
At home with the locals

INTERNET & WIFI

Almost every hotel, restaurant and café offers free WiFi for guests. *The Cloud* is a network with wide WiFi coverage that is free of charge. Register as a guest with your smartphone which automatically logs into the network.

MEDIA

The BBC is the gold standard, with its wide range of TV and radio programmes, while the second biggest TV broadcaster is ITV. The paid-for television service Sky is often found in pubs and hotels. National newspapers include *The Guardian* (left leaning), *The Times* and the *Telegraph* (both right leaning), and the *Financial Times*. *The Sun* and the *Daily Mirror* are both tabloid newspapers. The *Big Issue* is a widely available magazine sold on the street by homeless people.

MONEY & CREDIT CARDS

The British pound or sterling (GBP, £) is the currency – you will not get far in England with dollars. There are 100 pence in a pound. Credit and debit cards are widely accepted, even for small amounts. Contactless payment is popular with the relevant debit or credit cards as well as providers such as ApplePay. There are banks *(Mon–Fri 10am–5pm, sometimes also Sat in big cities)* in larger towns and ATMs even in small villages, often in grocery shops, fuel stations or pubs. Bureaux de change are good places to change money, especially those in post offices or *Marks & Spencer* department stores.

RESPONSIBLE TRAVEL

It doesn't take a lot to be environmentally friendly whilst travelling. Don't just think about your carbon footprint while flying to and from your holiday destination but also about how you can protect nature and culture abroad. As a tourist, it is especially important to respect nature, look out for local products, cycle instead of driving, save water and much more. If you would like to find out more about ecotourism, please visit: *ecotourism.org*.

OPENING HOURS

The main opening hours are Monday–Saturday 10am–5.30pm, but many grocery stores have longer opening hours. In major cities, there is usually a 24-hour supermarket. Retail outlets are often open until 7pm and 8pm. On Sundays, you can also go shopping in many places in Devon and Cornwall (usually 11am–4pm).

PHONE & MOBILE PHONE

Apart from some very remote coastal areas and small islands, mobile phone reception in Devon and Cornwall is good. The major providers are Vodafone, EE, Three and O2. All providers also offer pre-paid cards. Reasonable tariffs for these cards are offered by Virgin, Tesco, Sainsbury's and Three. The country code for England is 0044. The UK dial code for the USA and Canada is 001, for Australia 0061, and for Ireland 00353.

PUBLIC HOLIDAYS

1 January	New Year's Day
March/April	Good Friday
	Easter Monday
First Monday in May	May Day Holiday
Last Monday in May	Spring Bank Holiday
Last Monday in August	Summer Bank Holiday
25 December	Christmas Day
26 December	Boxing Day

TIPPING

In restaurants, depending on how happy you are with the service, it is usual to add about 10 per cent to the bill – unless a service charge has already been added. Tipping is not the norm in pubs. Hotel staff and taxi drivers will be happy to receive a small tip.

TOURIST INFORMATION

VisitBritain *(visitbritain.com)* is the official website for UK tourism. For information about Devon and Cornwall, go to *visitdevon.co.uk* and *visitcornwall.com*

WEIGHTS & MEASURES

1 inch = 2.54cm
1 foot = 12 inches = 30.48 cm
1 yard = 3 feet = 91.4 cm
1 mile = 1.61 km
1 acre = 4,047 m²=0.4047 hectares
1 pint = 0.568 litre
1 imperial gallon = 4.5 litres
1 US gallon = 3.8 litres
1 ounce = 28.35g
1 pound = 16 ounces = 453.6g

WEATHER IN PLYMOUTH

High season
Low season

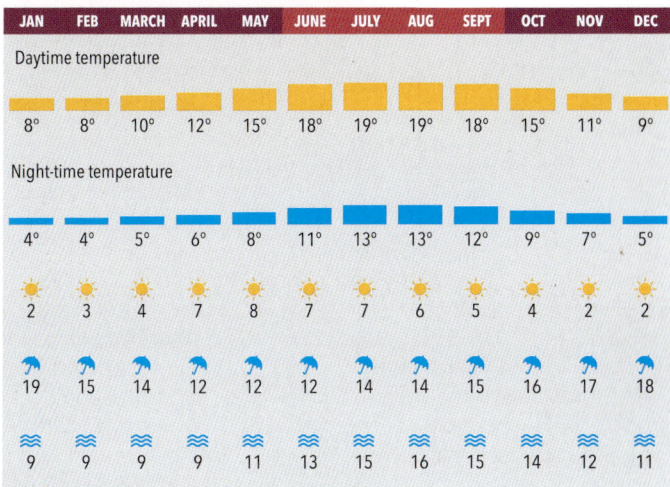

	JAN	FEB	MARCH	APRIL	MAY	JUNE	JULY	AUG	SEPT	OCT	NOV	DEC
Daytime temperature	8°	8°	10°	12°	15°	18°	19°	19°	18°	15°	11°	9°
Night-time temperature	4°	4°	5°	6°	8°	11°	13°	13°	12°	9°	7°	5°
Sunshine hours/day	2	3	4	7	8	7	7	6	5	4	2	2
Rainy days/month	19	15	14	12	12	12	14	14	15	16	17	18
Water temperature in °C	9	9	9	9	11	13	15	16	15	14	12	11

☀ Sunshine hours/day ☂ Rainy days/month ≈ Water temperature in °C

Longships Lighthouse stands on Carn Bras rock, some 2km off Land's End

HOLIDAY VIBES

FOR RELAXATION & CHILLING

FOR BOOKWORMS & FILM BUFFS

📖 IT'S TEATIME, MY DEAR

Bill Bryson's *Notes from a Small Island* (1995) is a true classic of travel literature. In *It's Teatime, My Dear* (2017), he travels once again through the country that feels both familiar and foreign to him. Short, witty episodes.

🎥 DOC MARTIN

A grumpy but brilliant surgeon from London becomes a GP in the depths of Cornwall. The doc is slow to warm to the new role and repeatedly causes offence with his direct manner. The TV series (ten seasons, 2004 to 2022) was filmed in Port Isaac.

📖 JAMAICA INN

Daphne du Maurier is said to have written this impressive pirates' novel (1936) during a stay at Jamaica Inn on Bodmin Moor. It's about shipwreckers, secrets and love. It inspired the film of the same name directed by Alfred Hitchcock.

🎥 FISHERMAN'S FRIENDS

In 2019, Chris Foggin brought the story of a sea-shanty choir from Port Isaac to the big screen: record producers discovered the group, and the singers became big stars, frequenting festival stages and even the Royal Albert Hall.

PLAYLIST ON SHUFFLE

⟳ ⏮ ⏸ ⏭ 🔊 ━━━━━━━━━━━━ 0:58

⏸ WILL KEATING – CORNWALL MY HOME
The singer's musical declaration of love for Cornwall, his home

▶ JAMES MORRISON – WONDERFUL WORLD
Morrison lived in Cornwall as a child, where he took his first steps as a musician – specifically in Newquay

▶ COLDPLAY – CLOCKS
Chris Martin, frontman of one of the most successful rock bands in the world, is from Exeter

▶ THE RUMBLE STRIPS – NOT THE ONLY PERSON
This rock band from Tavistock is popular at home and abroad

▶ SPECTRES – FAMILY
Loud indie rock from Devon, somewhere between Nirvana and Jesus & Mary Chain

Your holiday soundtrack can be found on **Spotify** under **MARCO POLO England**

Or scan this code with the Spotify app

ONLINE

THEGOODPUBGUIDE.CO.UK
The reference guide for pub lovers: *The Good Pub Guide* lists the country's best pubs – many of them happen to be in Devon and Cornwall.

ENGLISH HERITAGE DAYS OUT
This app provides maps, opening times and plenty of information to guide you round English Heritage sites (Android, iOS).

MET OFFICE
The free app from the official weather station, the Met Office, is very useful for planning your day. Usually correct (Android, iOS).

NATIONAL TRUST
The National Trust has a user-friendly app that enables you to search for attractions locally and nationwide (Android, iOS).

UK TIDES
Going to the beach? This app allows you to search for tide times in coastal locations throughout Britain (Android, iOS).

TRAVEL PURSUIT

THE MARCO POLO HOLIDAY QUIZ

Do you know what makes Devon and Cornwall tick? Test your knowledge of the idiosyncrasies and eccentricities of this region and its people. The answers are at the bottom of the page, with further details on pages 18 to 23 of this guide.

❶ Which natural phenomenon gives Devon and Cornwall their mild climate?
a) Foehn Wind
b) Gulf Stream
c) Balearic Low

❷ How much tea do Brits drink per person per year?
a) 5.36kg
b) 2.73kg
c) 1.94kg

❸ How much liquid constitutes a British pint?
a) 568ml
b) 473ml
c) 551ml

❹ How much should you tip at the bar in a pub?
a) £1
b) £2
c) Nothing

❺ What is the name of the iconic British landscape architect?
a) Leopold "Cateye" Green
b) Lancelot "Capability" Brown
c) Louis "Clematis" Black

❻ Which unit is used to measure speed in the UK?
a) Miles per hour
b) Kilometres per hour
c) Yards per hour

Answers: 1b, 2c, 3a, 4c, 5b, 6a, 7c, 8a, 9c, 10b, 11c, 12a

A Devon and Cornwall classic: but what makes up a cream tea?

❼ Which form of monarchy does the UK have?
a) Elected monarchy
b) Absolute monarchy
c) Constitutional monarchy

❽ Which city in Devon has a famous racecourse?
a) Exeter
b) Paignton
c) Ilfracombe

❾ What is the stone circle *Merry Maidens* meant to depict?
a) A group of 13 mermaids
b) A group of 15 brides
c) A group of 19 girls

❿ What belongs in a cream tea?
a) A slice of cream cake
b) A scone with jam and clotted cream
c) Bread with cream cheese

⓫ What does "MIF" mean in Devon and Cornwall?
a) A regional football club
b) A regional TV broadcaster in mid-Cornwall
c) It means drinking tea with the milk in first

⓬ Where was Rosamunde Pilcher born?
a) Lelant
b) Liskeard
c) Launceston

INDEX

Affinity Devon 8
Antony 118
Arlington Court 106
Barbara Hepworth
  Museum 56
Barnstaple 30, 107, 109
Beacon Cove 113
Bedruthan Steps 39, 59, 116
Bideford 98, 107, 109
Bigbury 35
Big Sheep, The 108
Bodmin 67, 123
Bodmin Moor 67, 68, 69
Boscastle 75
Bovey Castle 119
Braunton 109
Brixham 87
Bryher 54
Buckland Abbey 94
Bude 33, 75
Burgh Island 94
Calstock Viaduct 65
Camel Trail 32
Carbis Bay 57
Carnewas Island 116
Castle Drogo 95
Charlestown 42
Christie, Agatha 85, 89, 94,
  112–115, 123
Clovelly 110
Coldharbour Mill 104
Cornish language 16, 23
Cornwall Airport 15
Cotehele House 118
Dartmoor 15, 16, 33, 34, 76,
  94–97, 123
Dartmouth 34, 88, 114, 123
Dunster Castle 102
East Devon Area of
  Outstanding Natural
  Beauty 85
Eden Project 8, 42, 123
Exeter 15, 35, 76, 80–82,
  120, 121, 124, 131
Exmoor 15, 33, 34, 102–104,
  103, 123
Exmoor pony 99, 102
Exmouth 82
Exmouth Beach 11, 84
Falmouth 45, 123
Fowey 34, 69, 123
Geevor Tin Mine 52
Go Ape 10, 82
Godolphin 49
Granite Way 32, 97
Great Torrington 98, 109
Greenway 89, 114
Gribbin Head 71
Gulf Stream 14, 18

Hartland Coast 33, 111
Healeys Cornish Cyder
  Farm 45
Hidden Valley 64
Honiton 30
Hound Tor 94, 96
Hugh Town 53
Hurlers Stone Circles 22, 69
Ilfracombe 104–106, 107,
  109, 123
Isles of Scilly 16, 32, 33, 34,
  53–55
Jamaica Inn 69, 130
Jurassic Coast 84
Kents Cavern 8, 85
Kingswear 88, 114
Knightshayes 104
Kynance Cove 47
Land's End 16, 32, 38, 52
Lanhydrock 19, 69, 118
Lappa Valley Steam
  Railway 10, 59
Launceston 9, 64
Lawrence House 9, 64
Leisure World 8, 58
Lelant 21
Levant Mine 53
Liskeard 65
Lizard Peninsula 30, 47, 48
Lizard Point 16, 38, 47
Looe 67, 121, 123
Lost Gardens of Heligan 11,
  43, 117
Lostwithiel 30
Lundy Island 98, 106, 107
Lydford Castle 9, 97
Lydford Gorge 97
Lynmouth 102
Lynton 102, 109
Marisco Castle 107
Mawgan Porth 116
Merry Maidens 22
Mevagissey 43
Minack Theatre 51, 52
Moretonhampstead 95
National Marine Aquarium 8
Newlyn 35
Newquay 10, 11, 57–58, 116,
  121, 131
Newquay Zoo 10, 57
Okehampton 31, 97
Padstow 35, 71–72, 123
Paignton 28, 87, 114
Pendennis Castle 46
Penryn 35
Penzance 31, 49–50, 120,
  122
Plymouth 35, 91–93, 124,
  127

Poldark Mine 49
Polkerris Beach 70
Polperro 10, 67
Polruan 70
Porlock 11, 31, 102
Porthcothan Bay 116
Porthcurno 51
Porthleven 49, 123
Port Isaac 11, 61, 73, 130
Powderham Castle 82, 83
Restormel Castle 69
Rock 72
Roseland 46
Rosemoor 109
Route 27 32
Salcombe 32, 90, 123
Saltram 94
Sennen Cove 35, 52
Sidmouth 84
South West Coast Path 11,
  16, 33, 111, 115–117
Splashdown Quaywest 10, 87
St Agnes 45, 53
Start Point Lighthouse 90
St Austell 28, 42
St Catherine's Castle 70
St Erth 56
St Ives 28, 30, 55–57, 123
St Keverne 9, 47
St Mary's 53
St Mawes 45
St Michael's Mount 50
Swanpool Beach 46
Tamar Valley 65
Tarka Trail 108, 109
Tavistock 131
Tintagel 22, 74, 118
Torbay 123
Torquay 77, 85–87, 113, 114,
  123
Torre Abbey 85, 113
Tregothnan Estate 31, 68
Treguddick Distillery 65
Trelissick Garden 45
Trengwainton Garden 50
Trerice 58, 117
Tresco 19, 54
Trethevy Quoit 67
Truro 35, 43–44, 124
Valley of the Rocks 102
Watergate Bay 58, 116
Westward Ho! 108
Whitesand Bay 52
Widecombe-in-the-Moor 94,
  96
Woodlands 10, 89
Woolacombe Bay 106

WE WANT TO HEAR FROM YOU!

Did you have a great holiday? Is there something on your mind? Whatever it is, let us know! Whether you want to praise the guide, alert us to errors or give us a personal tip – MARCO POLO would be pleased to hear from you.

We do everything we can to provide the very latest information for your trip. Nevertheless, despite all of our authors' thorough research, errors can creep in. MARCO POLO does not accept any liability for this.

Please contact us by email:

sales@heartwoodpublishing.co.uk

PICTURE CREDITS

Cover photo: Newquay, Towan Beach (huber-images: P. Canali)
Photos: uber-images: P. Canali (6/7, 38/39, 56, 60/61), O. Fantuz (43), J. Foulkes (outer front flap, inner front flap/1, 48, 59, 90, 95, 96), A. Piai (84), M. Rellini (32/33, 66), R. Schmid (9, 20, 55), R. Taylor (2/3), S. Wasek (73, 105, 110, 130/131); Laif: A. Artz (86); Laif/Le Figaro Magazine: Rogery (89); Laif/Loop Images: C. Button (76/77), N. Cable (12/13), M. Gibson (52), C. Harris (24/25), C. Joiner (back flap, 98/99, 103, 108), S. Staszczuk (14/15); Laif/robertharding: A. Burton (23), D. Clapp (120/121), A. Copson (8), M. Nolan (11), E. Rooney (19); Look/age fotostock (51, 74); Look/robertharding (27, 68); mauritius images/Alamy: K. Birtland (71), I. Dagnall (44), K. Kaminski (30/31), C. Mannings (107), N. McAllister (31), K. Nicholson (132/133), J. Pearce (123); mauritius images/Cultura (10, 35), mauritius images/imagebroker: S. Gabriel (112/113); mauritius images/nature picture library/2020VISION: A. Mustard (46); mauritius images/robertharding (65); mauritius images/United Archives: De Agostini (26/27); picture-alliance/imagebroker: M. Olszewski (83); M. Pohl (135); Shutterstock: Stephen Rees (16), Laurence Berger (28), Rolf E. Staerk (119), Mick Blakey (128/129)

3rd Edition – fully revised and updated 2024
Worldwide Distribution: Heartwood Publishing Ltd, Bath, United Kingdom
www.heartwoodpublishing.co.uk

Author: Michael Pohl
Editor: Corinna Walkenhorsty
Picture editor: Anja Schlattere
Cartography: © 2023 KOMPASS-Karten GmbH, A-6020 Innsbruck; MAIRDUMONT, D-73751 Ostfildern (pp. 36–37, 114–115, 116, 119, outer jacket, folding map); © 2023 KOMPASS-Karten GmbH, A-6020 Innsbruck; DuMont Reiseverlag, D-73751 Ostfildern (pp. 104, 108, 112, inset folding map); 2023 KOMPASS-Karten GmbH, kompass.de using © OpenStreetMap Contributors, osm.org/copyright (pp. 26–27, 31, 41, 54–55, 66–67, 78–79)
Cover design and pull-out map cover design: bilekjaeger_Kreativagentur with Zukunftswerkstatt, Stuttgart
Page design: Langenstein Communication GmbH, Ludwigsburg

Heartwood Publishing credits:
Translated from the German by Rachel Farmer, Suzanne Kirkbright
Editors: Felicity Laughton, Kate Michell, Rosamund Sales
Prepress: Summerlane Books, Bath
Printed in India

MARCO POLO AUTHOR
MICHAEL POHL

It's the quirky little places that Michael Pohl is so fond of. When the journalist and author found his second home in the city of Bristol, he was repeatedly drawn away from the crowds and into the far reaches of the southwest: Devon and Cornwall. He still visits the region regularly – to hike, chat with people and, not least, replenish supplies of his favourite coffee.

DOS & DON'TS

HOW TO AVOID SLIP-UPS & BLUNDERS

DON'T JUMP THE QUEUE

Queuing is an essential part of British culture. Whether you're in the pub or at the bus stop, you should diligently line up and, if in doubt, let others go in front of you. Queue jumpers are heavily frowned upon.

DO TRY THE ALE

Real ale divides opinion. It is brewed from traditional ingredients and is non-carbonated. It may not be your cup of tea, but do give it a try – you can always start with half a pint.

DON'T TRAVEL ON BANK HOLIDAYS

On bank holiday weekends the roads in the southwest are as busy as they are during the summer holidays (July–September). Unless you don't mind the traffic jams, overcrowded beaches and lack of parking spaces, avoid travelling at these times.

DO DRIVE ON THE LEFT

Some foreign visitors tend to slip into driving on the right at some point, particularly on narrow country lanes without road markings. If you're coming from abroad, stick a note on the dashboard as a reminder. You might save a life!